Have A Little Faith

A True Story

Mitch Albom

W F HOWES LTD

This large print edition published in 2010 by
W F Howes Ltd
Unit 4, Rearsby Business Park, Gaddesby Lane,
Rearsby, Leicester LE7 4YH

1 3 5 7 9 10 8 6 4 2

First published in the United Kingdom in 2009
by Sphere

A CIP catalogue record for this book is available
from the British Library

ISBN 978-1-40745-660-7

Typeset by Palimpsest Book Production Limited,
Falkirk, Stirlingshire
Printed and bound in Great Britain
by MPG Books Ltd, Bodmin, Cornwall

FSC
Mixed Sources
Product group from well-managed
forests, controlled sources and
recycled wood or fiber
SA-COC-1565
www.fsc.org
© 1996 Forest Stewardship Council

AUTHOR'S NOTE

This story spans eight years. It was made possible by the cooperation of two unique men, Albert Lewis and Henry Covington – who shared their histories in great detail – as well as their families, children, and grandchildren, to whom the author expresses his eternal gratitude. All encounters and conversations are true events, although for purposes of the narrative, the time line has, on a few occasions, been squeezed, so that, for example, a discussion held in October of one year may be presented in November of the next.

Also, while this is a book about faith, the author can make no claim to being a religion expert, nor is this a how-to guide for any particular belief. Rather, it is written in hope that all faiths can find something universal in the story.

The cover was inspired by Albert Lewis's old prayer book, held together by rubber bands.

Per the tradition of tithing, one-tenth of the author's profits on every book sold will be donated to charity, including the church, synagogue, and homeless shelters in this story.

The author wishes to thank the readers of his previous books, and welcome new readers with much appreciation.

CONTENTS

AUTUMN

WINTER

FINALLY, A BOOK FOR MY FATHER, IRA ALBOM,
IN WHOM I HAVE ALWAYS BELIEVED.

IN THE BEGINNING . . .

In the beginning, there was a question.

'Will you do my eulogy?'

I don't understand, I said.

'My eulogy?' the old man asked again. 'When I'm gone.' His eyes blinked from behind his glasses. His neatly trimmed beard was gray, and he stood slightly stooped.

Are you dying? I asked.

'Not yet,' he said, grinning.

Then why—

'Because I think you would be a good choice. And I think, when the time comes, you will know what to say.'

Picture the most pious man you know. Your priest. Your pastor. Your rabbi. Your imam. Now picture him tapping you on the shoulder and asking you to say good-bye to the world on his behalf.

Picture the man who sends people off to heaven, asking you for his send-off to heaven.

'So?' he said. 'Would you be comfortable with that?'

★   ★   ★

In the beginning, there was another question.

'Will you save me, Jesus?'

This man was holding a shotgun. He hid behind trash cans in front of a Brooklyn row house. It was late at night. His wife and baby daughter were crying. He watched for cars coming down his block, certain the next set of headlights would be his killers.

'Will you save me, Jesus?' he asked, trembling. 'If I promise to give myself to you, will you save me tonight?'

Picture the most pious man you know. Your priest. Your pastor. Your rabbi. Your imam. Now picture him in dirty clothes, a shotgun in his hand, begging for salvation from behind a set of trash cans.

Picture the man who sends people off to heaven, begging not to be sent to hell.

'Please, Lord,' he whispered. 'If I promise . . .'

This is a story about believing in something and the two very different men who taught me how. It took a long time to write. It took me to churches and synagogues, to the suburbs and the city, to the 'us' versus 'them' that divides faith around the world.

And finally, it took me home, to a sanctuary filled with people, to a casket made of pine, to a pulpit that was empty.

In the beginning, there was a question.

It became a last request.

'Will you do my eulogy?'

And, as is often the case with faith, I thought I was being asked a favor, when in fact I was being given one.

SPRING

IT IS 1965 . . .

. . . and my father drops me off at Saturday morning services.

'You should go,' he tells me.

I am seven, too young to ask the obvious question: why should I go and he shouldn't? Instead I do as I am told, entering the temple, walking down a long corridor, and turning toward the small sanctuary, where the children's services are held.

I wear a white short-sleeved shirt and a clip-on tie. I pull open the wooden door. Toddlers are on the floor. Third-grade boys are yawning. Sixth-grade girls wear black cotton leotards, slouching and whispering.

I grab a prayer book. The seats in back are taken so I choose one up front. Suddenly the door swings open and the room goes silent.

The Man of God steps in.

He stalks like a giant. His hair is thick and dark. He wears a long robe, and when he speaks, his waving arms move the robe around like a sheet flipping in the wind.

He tells a Bible story. He asks us questions. He strides

7

across the stage. He draws close to where I am sitting. I feel a flush of heat. I ask God to make me invisible. Please, God, please.

It is my most fervent prayer of the day.

MARCH

THE GREAT TRADITION OF
RUNNING AWAY

Adam hid in the Garden of Eden. Moses tried to substitute his brother. Jonah jumped a boat and was swallowed by a whale.

Man likes to run from God. It's a tradition. So perhaps I was only following tradition when, as soon as I could walk, I started running from Albert Lewis. He was not God, of course, but in my eyes, he was the next closest thing, a holy man, a man of the cloth, the big boss, the head rabbi. My parents joined his congregation when I was an infant. I sat on my mother's lap as he delivered his sermons.

And yet, once I realized who he was – a Man of God – I ran. If I saw him coming down the hallway, I ran. If I had to pass his study, I ran. Even as a teenager, if I spotted him approaching, I ducked down a corridor. He was tall, six foot one, and I felt tiny in his presence. When he looked down through his black-rimmed glasses, I was certain he could view all my sins and shortcomings.

So I ran.

I ran until he couldn't see me anymore.

I thought about that as I drove to his house, on a morning after a rainstorm in the spring of 2000. A few weeks earlier, Albert Lewis, then eighty-two years old, had made that strange request of me, in a hallway after a speech I had given.

'Will you do my eulogy?'

It stopped me in my tracks. I had never been asked this before. Not by anyone – let alone a religious leader. There were people mingling all around, but he kept smiling as if it were the most normal question in the world, until I blurted out something about needing time to think about it.

After a few days, I called him up.

Okay, I said, I would honor his request. I would speak at his funeral – but only if he let me get to know him as a man, so I could speak of him as such. I figured this would require a few in-person meetings.

'Agreed,' he said.

I turned down his street.

To that point, all I really knew of Albert Lewis was what an audience member knows of a performer: his delivery, his stage presence, the way he held the congregation rapt with his commanding voice and flailing arms. Sure, we had once been closer. He had taught me as a child, and he'd officiated at family functions – my sister's wedding, my

10

grandmother's funeral. But I hadn't really been around him in twenty-five years. Besides, how much do you know about *your* religious minister? You listen to him. You respect him. But as a man? Mine was as distant as a king. I had never eaten at his home. I had never gone out with him socially. If he had human flaws, I didn't see them. Personal habits? I knew of none.

Well, that's not true. I knew of one. I knew he liked to sing. Everyone in our congregation knew this. During sermons, any sentence could become an aria. During conversation, he might belt out the nouns or the verbs. He was like his own little Broadway show.

In his later years, if you asked how he was doing, his eyes would crinkle and he'd raise a conductor's finger and croon:

> *'The old gray rabbi,*
> *ain't what he used to be,*
> *ain't what he used to be . . .'*

I pushed on the brakes. What was I doing? I was the wrong man for this job. I was no longer religious. I didn't live in this state. He was the one who spoke at funerals, not me. Who does a eulogy for the man who does eulogies? I wanted to spin the wheel around, make up some excuse.

Man likes to run from God.

But I was headed in the other direction.

11

MEET THE REB

I walked up the driveway and stepped on the mat, which was rimmed with crumbled leaves and grass. I rang the doorbell. Even that felt strange. I suppose I didn't think a holy man had a doorbell. Looking back, I don't know what I expected. It was a house. Where else would he live? A cave?

But if I didn't expect a doorbell, I surely wasn't ready for the man who answered it. He wore sandals with socks, long Bermuda shorts, and an untucked, short-sleeved, button-down shirt. I had never seen the Reb in anything but a suit or a long robe. That's what we called him as teenagers. 'The Reb.' Kind of like a superhero. The Rock. The Hulk. The Reb. As I mentioned, back then he was an imposing force, tall, serious, broad cheeks, thick eyebrows, a full head of dark hair.

'Hellooo, young man,' he said cheerily.

Uh, hi, I said, trying not to stare.

He seemed more slender and fragile up close. His upper arms, exposed to me for the first time, were thin and fleshy and dotted with age marks. His thick glasses sat on his nose, and he blinked several times, as if focusing, like an old scholar interrupted while getting dressed.

'Ennnnter,' he sang. '*Enn-trez!*'

His hair, parted on the side, was between gray and snowy white, and his salt-and-pepper Vandyke beard was closely trimmed, although I noticed a few spots he had missed shaving. He shuffled down the hall, me in tow behind, looking at his bony legs and taking small steps so as not to bump up on him.

How can I describe how I felt that day? I have since discovered, in the book of Isaiah, a passage in which God states:

> '*My thoughts are not your thoughts*
> *Neither are your ways my ways*
> *For as the heavens are higher than the earth*
> *So are my ways higher than your ways*
> *And my thoughts higher than your thoughts.*'

That was how I *expected* to feel – lower, unworthy. This was one of God's messengers. I should be looking up, right?

Instead, I baby-stepped behind an old man in socks and sandals. And all I could think of was how goofy he looked.

A LITTLE HISTORY

I should tell you why I shunned the eulogy task, where I was, religiously, when this whole story began. Nowhere, to be honest. You know how Christianity speaks of fallen angels? Or how the Koran mentions the spirit Iblis, exiled from heaven for refusing to bow to God's creation?

Here on earth, falling is less dramatic. You drift. You wander off.

I know. I did it.

Oh, I could have been pious. I had a million chances. They began when I was a boy in a middle-class New Jersey suburb and was enrolled, by my parents, in the Reb's religious school three days a week. I could have embraced that. Instead, I went like a dragged prisoner. Inside the station wagon (with the few other Jewish kids in our neighborhood) I stared longingly out the window as we drove away, watching my Christian friends play kickball in the street. *Why me?* I thought. During classes, the teachers gave out pretzel sticks, and I would dreamily suck the salt off until the bell rang, setting me free.

By age thirteen, again at my parents' urging, I

had not only gone through the requisite training to be bar mitzvahed, I had actually learned to chant from the Torah, the holy scrolls that contain the first five books of the Old Testament. I even became a regular reader on Saturday mornings. Wearing my only suit (navy blue, of course), I would stand on a wooden box in order to be tall enough to look over the parchment. The Reb would be a few feet away, watching as I chanted. I could have spoken with him afterward, discussed that week's Biblical portion. I never did. I just shook his hand after services, then scrambled into my dad's car and went home.

My high school years – once more, at my parents' insistence – were spent mostly in a private academy, where half the day was secular learning and the other half was religious. Along with algebra and European history, I studied Exodus, Deuteronomy, Kings, Proverbs, all in their original language. I wrote papers on arks and manna, Kabbalah, the walls of Jericho. I was even taught an ancient form of Aramaic so I could translate Talmudic commentaries, and I analyzed twelfth-century scholars like Rashi and Maimonides.

When college came, I attended Brandeis University, with a largely Jewish student body. To help pay my tuition, I ran youth groups at a temple outside of Boston.

In other words, by the time I graduated and went out into the world, I was as well versed in my religion as any secular man I knew.

And then?

And then I pretty much walked away from it.

It wasn't revolt. It wasn't some tragic loss of faith. It was, if I'm being honest, apathy. A lack of need. My career as a sportswriter was blossoming; work dominated my days. Saturday mornings were spent traveling to college football games, Sunday mornings to professional ones. I attended no services. Who had time? I was fine. I was healthy. I was making money. I was climbing the ladder. I didn't need to ask God for much, and I figured, as long as I wasn't hurting anyone, God wasn't asking much of me either. We had forged a sort of 'you go your way, I'll go mine' arrangement, at least in my mind. I followed no religious rituals. I dated girls from many faiths. I married a beautiful, dark-haired woman whose family was half-Lebanese. Every December, I bought her Christmas presents. Our friends made jokes. A Jewish kid married a Christian Arab. Good luck.

Over time, I honed a cynical edge toward overt religion. People who seemed too wild-eyed with the Holy Spirit scared me. And the pious hypocrisy I witnessed in politics and sports – congressmen going from mistresses to church services, football coaches breaking the rules, then kneeling for a team prayer – only made things worse. Besides, Jews in America, like devout Christians, Muslims, or sari-wearing Hindus, often bite their tongues, because there's this

16

nervous sense that somebody out there doesn't like you.

So I bit mine.

In fact, the only spark I kept aglow from all those years of religious exposure was the connection to my childhood temple in New Jersey. For some reason, I never joined another. I don't know why. It made no sense. I lived in Michigan – six hundred miles away.

I could have found a closer place to pray.

Instead, I clung to my old seat, and every autumn, I flew home and stood next to my father and mother during the High Holiday services. Maybe I was too stubborn to change. Maybe it wasn't important enough to bother. But as an unexpected consequence, a certain pattern went quietly unbroken:

I had one clergyman – and only one clergyman – from the day I was born.

Albert Lewis.

And he had one congregation.

We were both lifers.

And that, I figured, was all we had in common.

LIFE OF HENRY

At the same time I was growing up in the suburbs, a boy about my age was being raised in Brooklyn. One day, he, too, would grapple with his faith. But his path was different.

As a child, he slept with rats.

Henry Covington was the second-youngest of seven kids born to his parents, Willie and Wilma Covington. They had a tiny, cramped apartment on Warren Street. Four brothers slept in one room; three sisters slept in another.

The rats occupied the kitchen.

At night, the family left a pot of rice on the counter, so the rats would jump in and stay out of the bedrooms. During the day, Henry's oldest brother kept the rodents at bay with a BB gun. Henry grew up terrified of the creatures, his sleep uneasy, fearful of bites.

Henry's mother was a maid – she mostly worked for Jewish families – and his father was a hustler, a tall, powerful man who liked to sing around the house. He had a sweet voice, like Otis Redding, but on Friday nights he would shave in the mirror and croon 'Big Legged Woman,' and his wife would steam because she knew where he was going. Fights would break out. Loud and violent.

When Henry was five years old, one such drunken scuffle drew his parents outside, screaming and cursing. Wilma pulled a .22-caliber rifle and threatened to shoot her husband. Another man jumped in just as she pulled the trigger, yelling, 'No, Missus, don't do that!'

The bullet got him in the arm.

Wilma Covington was sent away to Bedford Hills, a maximum security prison for women. Two years. On weekends, Henry would go with his father to visit her. They would talk through glass.

'Do you miss me?' she would ask.

'Yes, Mama,' Henry would answer.

During those years, he was so skinny they fed him a butterscotch weight gain formula to put meat on his bones. On Sundays he would go to a neighborhood Baptist church where the reverend took the kids home afterward for ice cream. Henry liked that. It was his introduction to Christianity. The reverend spoke of Jesus and the Father, and while Henry saw pictures of what Jesus looked like, he had to from his own vision of God. He pictured a giant, dark cloud with eyes that weren't human. And a crown on its head.

At night, Henry begged the cloud to keep the rats away.

THE FILE ON GOD

As the Reb led me into his small home office, the subject of a eulogy seemed too serious, too awkward a pivot, as if a doctor and patient had just met, and now the patient had to remove all his clothes. You don't begin a conversation with 'So, what should I say about you when you die?'

I tried small talk. The weather. The old neighborhood. We moved around the room, taking a tour. The shelves were crammed with books and files. The desk was covered in letters and notes. There were open boxes everywhere, things he was reviewing or reorganizing or something.

'It feels like I've forgotten much of my life,' he said.

It could take another life to go through all this.

'Ah,' he laughed. 'Clever, clever!'

It felt strange, making the Reb laugh, sort of special and disrespectful at the same time. He was not, up close, the strapping man of my youth, the man who always looked so large from my seat in the crowd.

Here, on level ground, he seemed much smaller.

20

More frail. He had lost a few inches to old age. His broad cheeks sagged now, and while his smile was still confident, and his eyes still narrowed into a wise, thoughtful gaze, he moved with the practiced steps of a person who worried about falling down, mortality now arm in arm with him. I wanted to ask two words: how long?

Instead, I asked about his files.

'Oh, they're full of stories, ideas for sermons,' he said. 'I clip newspapers. I clip magazines.' He grinned. 'I'm a Yankee clipper.'

I spotted a file marked 'Old Age.' Another huge one was marked 'God.'

You have a file on God? I asked.

'Yes. Move that one down closer, if you don't mind.'

I stood on my toes and reached for it, careful not to jostle the others. I placed it on a lower shelf.

'Nearer, my God, to thee,' he sang.

Finally, we sat down. I flipped open a pad. Years in journalism had ingrained the semaphore of interviewing, and he nodded and blinked, as if understanding that something more formal had begun. His chair was a low-backed model with casters that allowed him to roll to his desk or a cabinet. Mine was a thick green leather armchair. Too cushy. I kept sinking into it like a child.

'Are you comfortable?' he asked.

Yes, I lied.

'Want to eat something?'

No, thanks.

'Drink?'

I'm good.

'Good.'

Okay.

I hadn't written down a first question. What would be the right first question? How do you begin to sum up a life? I glanced again at the file marked 'God,' which, for some reason, intrigued me (what would be *in* that file?), then I blurted out the most obvious thing you could ask a man of the cloth.

Do you believe in God?

'Yes, I do.'

I scribbled that on my pad.

Do you ever speak to God?

'On a regular basis.'

What do you say?

'These days?' He sighed, then half-sang his answer. 'These days I say, "God, I know I'm going to see you soon. And we'll have some nice conversations. But meanwhile, God, if you're gonna taaake me, take me already. And if you're gonna leeeave me here"' – he opened his hands and looked to the ceiling – '"maybe give me the strength to do what should be done."'

He dropped his hands. He shrugged. It was the first time I heard him speak of his mortality. And it suddenly hit me that this wasn't just some speaking request I had agreed to; that every question I would

ask this old man would add up to the one I didn't
have the courage to ask.

What should I say about you when you die?
'Ahh,' he sighed, glancing up again.
What? Did God answer you?
He smiled.
'Still waiting,' he said.

IT IS 1966 . . .

. . . and my grandmother is visiting. We have finished dinner. Plates are being put away.

'It's yahrzeit,' she tells my mother.

'In the cabinet,' my mother answers.

My grandmother is a short, stout woman. She goes to the cabinet, but at her height, the upper shelf is out of reach.

'Jump up there,' she tells me.

I jump.

'See that candle?'

On the top shelf is a little glass, filled with wax. A wick sticks up from the middle.

'This?'

'Careful.'

What's it for?

'Your grandfather.'

I jump down. I never met my grandfather. He died of a heart attack, after fixing a sink at a summer cottage. He was forty-two.

Was that his? I ask.

My mother puts a hand on my shoulder.

'We light it to remember him. Go play.'

I leave the room, but I sneak a look back, and I see

24

my mother and grandmother standing by the candle, mumbling a prayer.

Later – after they have gone upstairs – I return. All the lights are out, but the flame illuminates the countertop, the sink, the side of the refrigerator. I do not yet know that this is religious ritual. I think of it as magic. I wonder if my grandfather is in there, a tiny fire, alone in the kitchen, stuck in a glass.

I never want to die.

LIFE OF HENRY

The first time Henry Covington accepted Jesus as his personal savior, he was only ten, at a small Bible camp in Beaverkill, New York. For Henry, camp meant two weeks away from the traffic and chaos of Brooklyn. Here kids played outside, chased frogs, and collected peppermint leaves in jars of water and left them in the sun. At night the counselors added sugar and made tea.

One evening, a pretty, light-skinned counselor asked Henry if he'd like to pray with her. She was seventeen, slim and gentle-mannered; she wore a brown skirt, a white frilly blouse, her hair was in a ponytail, and to Henry she was so beautiful he lost his breath.

Yes, he said. He would pray with her.

They went outside the bunk.

'Your name is Henry and you are a child of God.'

'My name is Henry,' he repeated, 'and I am a child of God.'

'Do you want to accept Jesus Christ as your savior?' she said.

'Yes, I do,' he answered.

She took his hand.

'Are you confessing your sins?'

'Yes, I am.'

'Do you want Jesus to forgive your sins?'

'Yes.'

She leaned her forehead into his. Her voice lowered.

'Are you asking Jesus to come into your life?'

'I am asking him.'

'Do you want me to pray with you?'

'Yes,' he whispered.

It was warm outside. The summer sky was reddening to dusk. Henry felt the girl's soft forehead, her hand squeezing his, her whispered prayers so close to his ears. This surely was salvation. He accepted it with all his heart.

The next day, a friend of his got a BB gun, and they shot it at the frogs and tried to kill them.

APRIL

THE HOUSE OF PEACE

I drove the car slowly under a light spring drizzle. For our second meeting, I had asked to see the Reb at work, because knowing what to say after a man died included knowing how he labored, right?

It was strange driving through the New Jersey suburbs where I'd grown up. They were provincially middle-class back then; fathers worked, mothers cooked, church bells rang – and I couldn't wait to get out. I left high school after the eleventh grade, went to college up near Boston, moved to Europe, then New York, and never lived here again. It seemed too small for what I wanted to achieve in life, like being stuck wearing your grade school clothes. I had dreams of traveling, making foreign friends in foreign cities. I had heard the phrase 'citizen of the world.' I wanted to be one.

But here I was, in my early forties, back in my old hometown. I drove past a grocery store and saw a sign in a window that read 'Water Ice.' We used to love that stuff as kids, cherry-or lemon-flavored, ten cents for a small, a quarter for a large.

I never really found it anywhere else. I saw a man emerge licking a cup of it, and for a moment I wondered what my life would be like if I'd stayed here, lived here, licked water ice as an adult.

I quickly dismissed the thought. I was here for a purpose. A eulogy. When I was done, I would go home.

The parking lot was mostly empty. I approached the temple, with its tall glass archway, but I felt no nostalgia. This was not the prayer house of my youth. As with many suburban churches and synagogues, our congregation, Temple Beth Sholom (which translates to 'House of Peace'), had followed a migratory pattern. It began in one place and moved to another, growing larger as it chased after its members who, over the years, picked more affluent suburbs. I once thought churches and temples were like hills, permanent in location and singular in shape. The truth is, many go where the customers go. They build and rebuild. Ours had grown from a converted Victorian house in a residential neighborhood to a sprawling edifice with a spacious foyer, nineteen classrooms and offices, and a wall honoring the generous benefactors who'd made it possible.

Personally, I preferred the cramped brick building of my youth, where you smelled kitchen aromas when you walked in the back door. I knew every inch of that place. Even the mop closet, where we used to hide as kids.

Where I once hid from the Reb.

But what stays the same in life?

Now the Reb was waiting for me in the foyer, this time wearing a collared shirt and a sports coat. He greeted me with a personalized chorus of 'Hello, Dolly':

> 'Helllooo, Mitchell,
> Well, hellooo, Mitchell,
> It's so nice to have you back
> Where you belong . . .'

I pasted a smile on my face. I wasn't sure how long I would last with the musical theater thing.

I asked how he'd been doing. He mentioned dizzy spells. I asked if they were serious.

He shrugged.

'Let me put it this way,' he said. '*The old gray rabbi—*'

Ain't what he used to be, I said.

'Ah.'

I felt bad that I had interrupted him. Why was I so impatient?

We walked down the hallway toward his office. At this point, in semiretirement, his hours were strictly of his own choosing. He could stay at home if he wanted; no one would object.

But religion is built on ritual, and the Reb loved the ritual of going in to work. He had nurtured this congregation from a few dozen families in 1948 to more than a thousand families today. I got the feeling the place had actually grown too big for his liking. There were too many members he didn't know personally. There were also other rabbis now – one senior, one assistant – who handled the day-to-day duties. The idea of assistants when the Reb first arrived would have been laughable. He used to carry the keys and lock the place up himself.

'Look.'

He pointed to a stack of wrapped presents inside a doorway.

What's that? I asked.

'The bride's room. They come here to get dressed before the wedding.'

He ran his eyes up and down the gifts and smiled.

'Lovely, isn't it?'

What?

'Life,' he said.

IT IS 1967 . . .

. . .and the houses are decorated for Christmas. Our neighborhood is mostly Catholic.

One morning, after a snowfall, a friend and I walk to school, wearing hooded jackets and rubber boots. We come upon a small house with a life-sized nativity scene on its front lawn.

We stop. We study the figures. The wise men. The animals.

Is that one Jesus? I ask.

'What one?'

The one standing up. With the crown.

'I think that's his father.'

Is Jesus the other guy?

'Jesus is the baby.'

Where?

'In the crib, stupid.'

We strain our necks. You can't see Jesus from the sidewalk.

'I'm gonna look,' my friend says.

You better not.

'Why?'

You can get in trouble.

I don't know why I say this. Already, at that age,

I sense the world as 'us' and 'them.' If you're Jewish, you're not supposed to talk about Jesus or maybe even look at Jesus.

'I'm looking anyhow,' my friend says.

I step in nervously behind him. The snow crunches beneath our feet. Up close, the figures of the three wise men seem phony, hardened plaster with orangey painted flesh.

'That's him,' my friend says.

I peer over his shoulder. There, inside the crib, is the baby Jesus, lying in painted hay. I shiver. I half expect him to open his eyes and yell, 'Gotcha!'

Come on, we're gonna be late, I say, backpedaling.

My friend sneers.

'Chicken,' he says.

LIFE OF HENRY

Having been taught to believe in the Father, and having accepted the Son as his personal savior, Henry took the Holy Ghost to heart, for the first time, when he was twelve years old, on a Friday night at the True Deliverance Church in Harlem.

It was a Pentecostal tarry service – inspired by Jesus' call to tarry in the city until 'endued with a power from on high' – and as part of the tradition, people were called to receive the Holy Spirit. Henry followed others up to the pulpit, and when his turn came, he was swabbed with olive oil, then told to get on his knees and lean over a newspaper.

'Call him,' he heard voices say.

So Henry called. He said 'Jesus' and 'Jesus' and then 'Jesus, Jesus, Jesus,' over and over, until the words tumbled one into another. He swayed back and forth and spoke the name repeatedly. Minutes passed. His knees began to ache.

'Jesus, Jesus, Jesus, Jesus . . .'

'Call him!' the church members hollered. 'Call on him!'

'*Jesus-Jesus-Jesus-Jesus-Jesus*—'

'It's coming! Call him now!'

His head was pounding. His shins cramped in pain.

'*JesusJesusJesusJesusJesusJesusJesusJesusJesus Jesus*—'

'Almost! Almost!'

'Call him! Call him!'

He was sweating, choking, fifteen minutes, maybe twenty. Finally the words were so tumbled and bumbled that it didn't sound like 'Jesus' anymore, just syllables and gurgling and mumbling and groaning and saliva drooling from his mouth onto the newspaper. His voice and tongue and teeth and lips were melded into a shaking machine, gone wild with frenzy—

'*JelesulsjesleuesJesuslelelajJelsusu*—'

'You got it! He got it!'

And he had it. Or he thought he had it. He exhaled and he heaved and he almost choked. He took a big breath and tried to calm himself down. He wiped his chin. Someone balled up the wet newspaper and took it away.

'How do you feel now?' the pastor asked him.

'Good,' Henry panted.

'You feel good that He has given you the Holy Ghost?'

And he did. Feel good. Although he wasn't really sure what he'd done. But the pastor smiled and asked the Lord to protect Henry and that was mostly what he wanted, a prayer of protection.

It made him feel safe when he returned to his neighborhood.

Henry ingested the Holy Ghost that night. But soon he ingested other things, too. He started smoking cigarettes. He tried alcohol. He got tossed out of the sixth grade for fighting with a girl, and soon he added marijuana to his list.

One time, as a teenager, he heard his mother talking to relatives about how, of all her children, Henry was the one, he had the heart and the temperament. Her little boy was 'gonna be a preacher one day.'

And Henry laughed to himself. 'A preacher? Do you know how much of this stuff I'm smoking?'

THE DAILY GRIND OF FAITH

The Reb's office at work was not much different than the home version. Messy. Sprawling. Papers. Letters. Souvenirs. And a sense of humor. On the door was a list of blessings, some funny posters, even a mock parking sign that read:

YOU TAKA MY SPACE
I BREAKA YOUR FACE.

Once we sat, I cleared my throat. My question was simple. Something one would certainly need to know to construct a proper eulogy.

Why did you get into this business?

'This business?'

Religion.

'Ah.'

Did you have a calling?

'I wouldn't say so, no.'

There wasn't a vision? A dream? God didn't come to you in some shape or form?

'I think you've been reading too many books.'

Well. The Bible.

He grinned. 'I am not in that one.'

I meant no disrespect. It's just that I had always felt that rabbis, priests, pastors, any cleric, really, lived on a plane between mortal ground and heavenly sky. God up there. Us down here. Them in between.

This was easy to believe with the Reb, at least when I was younger. In addition to his imposing presence and his brilliant reputation, there were his sermons. Delivered with passion, humor, roaring indignation or stirring whispers, the sermon, for Albert Lewis, was like the fastball for a star pitcher, like the aria for Pavarotti. It was the reason people came; we knew it – and deep down, I think he knew it. I'm sure there are congregations where they slip out before the sermon begins. Not ours. Wristwatches were glanced at and footsteps hurried when people thought they might be late for the Reb's message.

Why? I guess because he didn't approach the sermon in a traditional way. I would later learn that, while he was trained in a formal, academic style – start at point A, move to point B, provide analysis and supporting references – after two or three tries in front of people, he gave up. They were lost. Bored. He saw it on their faces.

So he began with the first chapter of Genesis, broke it down to the simplest of ideas and related them to everyday life. He asked questions. He took questions. And a new style was born.

Over the years, those sermons morphed into gripping performances. He spoke with the cues of a magician, moving from one crescendo to the next, mixing in a Biblical quotation, a Sinatra song, a vaudeville joke, Yiddish expressions, even calling, on occasion, for audience participation ('Can I get a volunteer?'). Anything was fair game. There was a sermon where he pulled up a stool and read Dr Seuss's *Yertle the Turtle*. There was a sermon where he sang 'Those Were the Days.' There was a sermon where he brought a squash and a piece of wood, then slammed each with a knife to show that things which grow quickly are often more easily destroyed than those which take a long time.

He might quote *Newsweek, Time,* the *Saturday Evening Post*, a *Peanuts* cartoon, Shakespeare, or the TV series *Matlock*. He'd sing in English, in Hebrew, in Italian, or in a mock Irish accent; pop songs, folk songs, ancient songs. I learned more about the power of language from the Reb's sermons than from any book I ever read. You could glance around the room and see how no one looked away; even when he was scolding them, they were riveted. Honestly, you exhaled when he finished, that's how good he was.

Which is why, given his profession, I wondered if he'd been divinely inspired. I remembered Moses and the burning bush; Elijah and the still, small voice; Balaam and the donkey; Job and the whirlwind. To preach holy words, I assumed, one must have had some revelation.

'It doesn't always work that way,' the Reb said.

So what drew you in?

'I wanted to be a teacher.'

A religious teacher?

'A history teacher.'

Like in normal school?

'Like in normal school.'

But you went to the seminary.

'I tried.'

You tried?

'The first time, I failed.'

You're kidding me.

'No. The head of the seminary, Louis Finkelstein, pulled me aside and said, "Al, while you know much, we do not feel you have what it takes to be a good and inspiring rabbi."'

What did you do?

'What could I do? I left.'

Now, this stunned me. There were many things you could have said about Albert Lewis. But not having what it took to inspire and lead a congregation? Unthinkable. Maybe he was too gentle for the seminary leaders. Or too shy. Whatever the reason, the failure crushed him.

He took a summer job as a camp counselor in Port Jervis, New York. One of the campers was particularly difficult. If the other kids collected in one place, this kid went some-place else. If asked to sit, he would defiantly stand.

The kid's name was Phineas, and Al spent most of the summer encouraging him, listening to his problems, smiling patiently. Al understood adolescent angst. He'd been a pudgy teen in a cloistered religious environment. He'd had few friends. He'd never really dated.

So Phineas found a kindred soul in his counselor. And by the end of camp, the kid had changed.

A few weeks later, Al got a call from Phineas's father, inviting him to dinner. It turned out the man was Max Kadushin, a great Jewish scholar and a major force in the Conservative movement. At the table that night, he said, 'Al, I can't thank you enough. You sent back a different kid. You sent me a young man.'

Al smiled.

'You have a way with people – particularly children.'

Al said thank you.

'Have you ever thought about trying for the seminary?'

Al almost spit out his food.

'I did try,' he said. 'I didn't make it.'

Max thought for a moment.

'Try again,' he said.

And with Kadushin's help, Albert Lewis's second try went better than the first. He excelled. He was ordained.

Not long after that, he took a bus to New Jersey to interview for his first and only pulpit position, the one he still held more than fifty years later.

No angel? I asked. No burning bush?

'A bus,' the Reb said, grinning.

I scribbled a note. The most inspirational man I knew only reached his potential by helping a child reach his.

As I left his office, I tucked away the yellow pad. From our meetings I now knew he believed in God, he spoke to God, he became a Man of God sort of by accident, and he was good with kids. It was a start.

We walked to the lobby. I looked around at the big building I usually saw once a year.

'It's good to come home, yes?' the Reb said.

I shrugged. It wasn't my home anymore.

Is it okay, I asked, to tell these stories, when I . . . you know . . . do the eulogy?

He stroked his chin.

'When that time comes,' he said, 'I think you'll know what to say.'

LIFE OF HENRY

When Henry was fourteen, his father died after a long illness. Henry wore a suit to the funeral home, because Willie Covington insisted all his sons have suits, even if there was no money for anything else.

The family approached the open coffin. They stared at the body. Willie had been extremely dark-skinned, but the parlor had made him up to be an auburn shade. Henry's oldest sister began to wail. She started wiping off the makeup, screaming, 'My daddy don't look like that!' Henry's baby brother tried to crawl into the coffin. His mother wept.

Henry watched quietly. He only wanted his father back.

Before God, Jesus, or any higher power, Henry had worshipped his dad, a former mattress maker from North Carolina who stood six foot five and had a chest full of gunshot scars, the details of which were never explained to his children. He was a tough man who chain-smoked and liked to drink, but when he came home at night, inebriated, he was often tender, and he'd call Henry over and say, 'Do you love your daddy?'

'Yeah,' Henry would say.

'Give your daddy a hug now. Give your daddy a kiss.'

Willie was an enigma, a man with no real job who was a stickler for education, a hustler and loan shark who forbade stolen goods in his house. When Henry began smoking in the sixth grade, his father's only response was: 'Don't never ask *me* for a cigarette.'

But Willie loved his children, and he challenged them, quizzing them on school subjects, offering a dollar for easy questions, ten dollars for a math problem. Henry loved to hear him sing – especially the old spirituals, like 'It's Cool Down Here by the River Jordan.'

But soon his singing stopped. Willie hacked and coughed. He developed emphysema and tuberculosis of the brain. In the last year of his life, he was virtually bedridden. Henry cooked his meals and carried them to his room, even as his father coughed up blood and barely ate a thing.

One night, after Henry brought him dinner, his father looked at him sadly and rasped, 'Listen, son, you ever run out of cigarettes, you can have some of mine.'

A few weeks later, he was dead.

At the funeral, Henry heard a Baptist preacher say something about the soul and Jesus, but not much got through. He kept thinking his father would come back, just show up at the door one day, singing his favorite songs.

Months passed. It didn't happen.

Finally, having lost his only hero, Henry, the hustler's son, made a decision: from now on, he would take what he wanted.

MAY

RITUAL

Spring was nearly over, summer on its way, and the late morning sun burned hot through the kitchen window. It was our third visit. Before we began, the Reb poured me a glass of water.

'Ice?' he asked.

I'm okay, I said.

'He's okay,' he sang. 'No ice . . . it would be nice . . . but no ice . . .'

As we walked back to his office, we passed a large photo of him as a younger man, standing on a mountain in bright sunlight. His body was tall and strong, his hair black and combed back – the way I remembered him from childhood.

Nice photo, I said.

'That was a proud moment.'

Where was it?

'Mount Sinai.'

Where the Ten Commandments were given?

'Exactly.'

When was this?

'In the 1960s. I was traveling with a group of scholars. A Christian man and I climbed up. He took that picture.'

46

How long did it take?

'Hours. We climbed all night and arrived at sunrise.'

I glanced at his aging body. Such a trip would be impossible now. His narrow shoulders were hunched over, and the skin at his wrists was wrinkled and loose.

As he walked on to his office, I noticed a small detail in the photo. Along with his white shirt and a prayer shawl, the Reb was wearing the traditional *tefillin*, small boxes containing Biblical verses, which observant Jews strap around their heads and their arms while reciting morning prayers.

He said he climbed all night.

Which meant he had taken them up with him.

Such ritual was a major part of the Reb's life. Morning prayers. Evening prayers. Eating certain foods. Denying himself others. On Sabbath, he walked to synagogue, rain or shine, not operating a car, as per Jewish law. On holidays and festivals, he took part in traditional practices, hosting a Seder meal on Passover, or casting bread into a stream on Rosh Hashanah, symbolic of casting away your sins.

Like Catholicism, with its vespers, sacraments, and communions – or Islam, with its five-times-daily *salah*, clean clothes, and prayer mats – Judaism had enough rituals to keep you busy all day, all week, and all year.

I remember, as a kid, the Reb admonishing the congregation – gently, and sometimes not so gently – for letting rituals lapse or disappear, for eschewing traditional acts like lighting candles or saying blessings, even neglecting the Kaddish prayer for loved ones who had died.

But even as he pleaded for a tighter grip, year after year, his members opened their fingers and let a little more go. They skipped a prayer here. They skipped a holiday there. They intermarried – as I did.

I wondered, now that his days were dwindling, how important ritual still was.

'Vital,' he said.

But why? Deep inside, you know your convictions.

'Mitch,' he said, 'faith is about doing. You are how you act, not just how you believe.'

Now, the Reb didn't merely practice his rituals; he carved his daily life from them. If he wasn't praying, he was studying – a major part of his faith – or doing charity or visiting the sick. It made for a more predictable life, perhaps even a dull one by American standards. After all, we are conditioned to reject the 'same old routine.' We're supposed to keep things new, fresh. The Reb wasn't into fresh. He never took up fads. He didn't do Pilates, he didn't golf (someone gave him a single club once; it sat in his garage for years).

But there was something calming about his pious

life, the way he puttered from one custom to the next; the way certain hours held certain acts; the way every autumn he built a *sukkah* hut with its roof open to the stars; the way every week he embraced the Sabbath, breaking the world down to six days and one day, six days and one.

'My grandparents did these things. My parents, too. If I take the pattern and throw it out, what does that say about their lives? Or mine? From generation to generation, these rituals are how we remain . . .'

He rolled his hand, searching for the word.

Connected? I said.

'Ah.' He smiled at me. 'Connected.'

THE END OF SPRING

As we walked to the front door that day, I felt a wave of guilt. I'd once had rituals; I'd ignored them for decades. These days, I didn't do a single thing that tied me to my faith. Oh, I had an exciting life. Traveled a lot. Met interesting people. But my daily routines – work out, scan the news, check e-mail – were self-serving, not roped to tradition. To what was I connected? A favorite TV show? The morning paper? My work demanded flexibility. Ritual was the opposite.

Besides, I saw religious customs as sweet but outdated, like typing with carbon paper. To be honest, the closest thing I had to a religious routine was visiting the Reb. I had now seen him at work and at home, in laughter and in repose. I had seen him in Bermuda shorts.

I had also seen him more this one spring than I normally would in three years. I still didn't get it. I was one of those disappointing congregants. Why had he chosen me to be part of his death, when I had probably let him down in life?

We reached the door.

50

One more question, I said.

'One mooore,' he sang, 'at the doooor . . .'

How do you not get cynical?

He stopped.

'There is no room for cynicism in this line of work.'

But people are so flawed. They ignore ritual, they ignore faith – they even ignore you. Don't you get tired of trying?

He studied me sympathetically. Maybe he realized what I was really asking: *Why me?*

'Let me answer with a story,' he said. 'There's this salesman, see? And he knocks on a door. The man who answers says, 'I don't need anything today.'

'The next day, the salesman returns.

'"Stay away," he is told.

'The next day, the salesman is back.

'The man yells, 'You again! I warned you!' He gets so angry, he spits in the salesman's face.

'The salesman smiles, wipes the spit with a handkerchief, then looks to the sky and says, "Must be raining."

'Mitch, that's what faith is. If they spit in your face, you say it must be raining. But you still come back tomorrow.'

He smiled.

'So, you'll come back, too? Maybe not *tomorrow* . . .'

He opened his arms as if expecting an incoming package. And for the first time in my life, I did the opposite of running away.

I gave him a hug.

It was a fast one. Clumsy. But I felt the sharp bones in his back and his whiskered cheek against mine. And in that brief embrace, it was as if a larger-than-life Man of God was shrinking down to human size.

I think, looking back, that was the moment the eulogy request turned into something else.

SUMMER

IT IS 1971 . . .

I am thirteen. This is the big day. I lean over the holy
scrolls, holding a silver pointer; its tip is the shape
of a hand. I follow the ancient text, chanting the
words. My teenage voice squeaks.

In the front row sit my parents, siblings, and grandparents. Behind them, more family, friends, the kids
from school.

Just look down, I tell myself. Don't mess up.

I go on for a while. I do pretty well. When I am
finished, the group of men around me shake my wet
hand. They mumble, 'Yishar co-ach' – *congratula-
tions* – and then I turn and take the long walk across
the pulpit to where the Reb, in his robe, stands
waiting.

He looks down through his glasses. He motions for
me to sit. The chair seems huge. I spot his prayer book,
which has clippings stuffed in the pages. I feel like I
am inside his private lair. He sings loudly and I sing,
too – also loudly, so he won't think I am slacking –
but my bones are actually trembling. I am finished
with the obligatory part of my Bar Mitzvah, but
nothing is as unsettling as what is about to come: the
conversation with the rabbi. You cannot study for this.

It is free-form. Worst of all, you have to stand right next to him. No running from God.

When the prayer finishes, I rise. I barely reach above the lectern, and some congregants have to shift to see me.

'So, how are you feeling, young man?' the Reb says. 'Relieved?'

Yeah, I mumble.

I hear muffled laughter from the crowd.

'When we spoke a few weeks ago, I asked you what you thought about your parents. Do you remember?'

Sort of, I say.

More laughter.

'I asked if you felt they were perfect, or if they needed improvement. And do you remember what you said?'

I freeze.

'You said they weren't perfect, but . . .'

He nods at me. Go ahead. Speak.

But they don't need improvement? I say.

'But they don't need improvement,' he says. 'This is very insightful. Do you know why?'

No, I say.

More laughter.

'Because it means you are willing to accept people as they are. Nobody is perfect. Not even Mom and Dad. That's okay.'

He smiles and puts two hands on my head. He recites a blessing. 'May the Lord cause his countenance to shine upon you . . .'

So now I am blessed. The Lord shines on me.

Does that mean I get to do more stuff, or less?

LIFE OF HENRY

About the time that, religiously, I was becoming 'a man,' Henry was becoming a criminal.

He began with stolen cars. He played lookout while his older brother jimmied the locks. He moved on to purse snatching, then shoplifting, particularly grocery stores; stealing pork chop trays and sausages, hiding them in his oversized pants and shirts.

School was a lost cause. When others his age were going to football games and proms, Henry was committing armed robbery. Young, old, white, black, didn't matter. He waved a gun and demanded their cash, their wallets, their jewels.

The years passed. Over time, he made enemies on the streets. In the fall of 1976, a neighborhood rival tried to set him up in a murder investigation. The guy told the cops Henry was the killer. Later, he said it was someone else.

Still, when those cops came to question him, Henry, now nineteen years old with a sixth-grade education, figured he could turn the tables on his rival and collect a five-thousand-dollar reward in the process.

So instead of saying 'I have no idea' or 'I was nowhere near there,' he made up lies about who was where, who did what. He made up one lie after another. He put himself at the scene, but not as a participant. He thought he was being smart.

He couldn't have been dumber. He wound up lying his way into an arrest – along with another guy – on a manslaughter charge. The other guy went to trial, was convicted, and got sent away for twenty-five years. Henry's lawyer quickly recommended a plea deal. Seven years. Take it.

Henry was devastated. Seven years? For a crime he didn't commit?

'What should I do?' he asked his mother.

'Seven is less than twenty-five,' she said.

He fought back tears. He took the deal in a courtroom. He was led away in handcuffs.

On the bus ride to prison, Henry cursed the fact that he was being punished unfairly. He didn't do the math on the times he could have been jailed and wasn't. He was angry and bitter. And he swore that life would owe him once he got out.

THE THINGS WE LOSE . . .

It was now the summer of 2003, and we were in the kitchen. His wife, Sarah, had cut up a honeydew, and the Reb, wearing a white short-sleeved shirt, red socks, and sandals – these combinations no longer startled me – held out a plate.

'Eat some,' he said.

In a bit.

'You're not hungry?'

In a bit.

'It's good for you.'

I ate a piece.

'You *liiike*?'

I rolled my eyes. He was clowning with me. I never thought I'd still be coming, three years after our visits began. When someone asks for a eulogy, you suspect the end is near.

But the Reb, I'd learned, was like a tough old tree; he bent with the storms but he would not snap. Over the years, he had beaten back Hodgkin's disease, pneumonia, irregular heart rhythms, and a small stroke.

These days, to safeguard his now eighty-five-year-old body, he took a daily gulping of pills, including Dilantin for seizure control, and Vasotec and Toprol for his heart and his blood pressure. He had recently endured a bout with shingles. Not long before this visit, he had tumbled, fractured his rib cage, and spent a few days in the hospital, where his doctor implored him to use a cane everywhere – 'For your own safety,' the doctor said. He rarely did, thinking the congregation might see him as weak.

But whenever I showed up, he was raring to go. And I was privately happy he fought his body's decay. I did not like seeing him frail. He had always been this towering figure, a tall and upright Man of God.

Selfishly, that's how I wanted him to stay.

Besides, I had witnessed the alternative. Eight years earlier, I'd watched an old and beloved professor of mine, Morrie Schwartz, slowly die of ALS. I visited him on Tuesdays in his home outside Boston. And every week, although his spirit shone, his body decayed.

Less than eight months from our first visit, he was dead.

I wanted Albert Lewis – who was born the same year as Morrie – to last longer. There were so many things I never got to ask my old professor. So many times I told myself, 'If I only had a few more minutes . . .'

60

I looked forward to my encounters with the Reb – me sitting in the big green chair, him searching hopelessly for a letter on his desk. Some visits, I would fly straight from Detroit to Philadelphia. But mostly I came on Sunday mornings, taking a train from New York City after filming a TV show there. I arrived during church hours, so I guess this was our own little church time, if you can refer to two Jewish men talking religion as church.

My friends reacted with curiosity or disbelief.
'You go to his house like he's a normal person?'
'Aren't you intimidated?'
'Does he make you pray while you're there?'
'You actually talk about his eulogy? Isn't that morbid?'

I guess, looking back, it wasn't the most normal thing. And after a while, I could have stopped. I certainly had enough material for an homage.

But I felt a need to keep visiting, to ensure that my words would still reflect who he was. And, okay. There was more. He had stirred up something in me that had been dormant for a long time. He was always celebrating what he called 'our beautiful faith.' When others said such things, I felt uneasy, not wanting to be lumped in with any group that closely. But seeing him so – what's the word? – joyous, I guess, at his age, was appealing. Maybe the faith didn't mean that much to me, but it did to him, you could

61

see how it put him at peace. I didn't know many people at peace.

So I kept coming. We talked. We laughed. We read through his old sermons and discussed their relevance. I found I could share almost anything with Reb. He had a way of looking you in the eye and making you feel the world had stopped and you were all that was in it.

Maybe this was his gift to the job.

Or maybe it was the job's gift to him.

Anyhow, he did a lot more listening these days. With his retirement from the senior rabbi position, the meetings and paperwork had decreased. Unlike when he first arrived, the temple ran quite well on its own now.

The truth is, he could have retired to someplace warm – Florida, Arizona. But that was never for him. He attended a retirees' convention in Miami once and was perplexed at how many former colleagues he discovered living there.

'Why did you leave your congregations?' he asked.

They said it hurt not to be up on the pulpit or the new clerics didn't like them hanging around.

The Reb – who often said 'ego' was the biggest threat to a clergyman – held no such envy for where he'd once been. Upon retirement, he voluntarily moved out of his large office and into a smaller one. And one Sabbath morning, he left his favorite chair on the dais and took a seat beside his wife in the back row of the sanctuary. The congregation was stunned.

But like John Adams returning to the farm after the presidency, the Reb simply faded back in among the people.

FROM A SERMON BY THE REB, 1958

'A little girl came home from school with a drawing she'd made in class. She danced into the kitchen, where her mother was preparing dinner.

'"Mom, guess what?" she squealed, waving the drawing.

'Her mother never looked up.

'"What?" she said, tending to the pots.

'"Guess what?" the child repeated, waving the drawing.

'"What?" the mother said, tending to the plates.

'"Mom, you're not listening."

'"Sweetie, yes I am."

'"Mom," the child said, "you're not listening with your *eyes*."'

LIFE OF HENRY

His first stop behind bars was Rikers Island, in the East River near the runways at LaGuardia Airport. It was painfully close to home, just a few miles, and it only reminded him how his stupidity had put him on the wrong side of these walls.

During his time at Rikers, Henry saw things he wished he'd never seen. He saw inmates assault and abuse other inmates, throwing blankets over the victims' heads so they couldn't see their attackers. One day, a guy who'd had an argument with Henry entered the room and punched Henry in the face. Two weeks later, the same man tried to stab Henry with a sharpened fork.

All this time, Henry wanted to scream his innocence, but what good would it do? Everybody screamed innocence. After a month or so, Henry was sent upstate to Elmira Correctional, a maximum security prison. He rarely ate. He barely slept. He smoked endless cigarettes. One hot night he woke up sweating, and rose to get himself a cold drink. Then the sleep faded and he saw the steel door. He dropped onto his bed and wept.

Henry asked God that night why he hadn't died as a baby. A light flickered and caught his eye and his gaze fell on a Bible. He opened it to a page from the Book of Job, where Job curses the day of his birth.

It was the first time he ever felt the Lord talking to him.

But he didn't listen.

JUNE

COMMUNITY

Having finished the honeydew, the Reb and I moved to his office, where the boxes, papers, letters, and files were still in a state of chaos. Had he felt better, we might have gone for a walk, because he liked to walk around his neighborhood, although he admitted not knowing his neighbors so well these days.

'When I was growing up in the Bronx,' the Reb said, 'everyone knew everyone. Our apartment building was like family. We watched out for one another.

'I remember once, as a boy, I was so hungry, and there was a fruit and vegetable truck parked by our building. I tried to bump against it, so an apple would fall into my hands. That way it wouldn't feel like stealing.

'Suddenly, I heard a voice from above yelling at me in Yiddish, '*Albert, it is forbidden!*' I jumped. I thought it was God.'

Who was it? I asked.

'A lady who lived upstairs.'

I laughed. Not quite God.

'No. But, Mitch, we were part of each other's

lives. If someone was about to slip, someone else could catch him.

'That's the critical idea behind a congregation. We call it a *Kehillah Kedoshah* – a sacred community. We're losing that now. The suburbs have changed things. Everyone has a car. Everyone has a million things scheduled. How can you look out for your neighbor? You're lucky to get a family to sit down for a meal together.'

He shook his head. The Reb was generally a move-with-the-times guy. But I could tell he didn't like this form of progress at all.

Still, even in retirement, the Reb had a way of stitching together his own sacred community. Day after day, he would peer through his glasses at a scribbled address book and punch telephone numbers. His home phone, a gift from his grand-children, had giant black-and-white digits, so he could dial more easily.

'Hellooo,' he'd begin, 'this is Albert Lewis calling for . . .'

He kept track of people's milestones – an anniversary, a retirement – and called. He kept track of who was sick or ailing – and called. He listened patiently as people went on and on about their joys or worries.

He took particular care to call his oldest congregants, because, he said, 'It makes them still feel a part of things.'

I wondered if he wasn't talking about himself.

★   ★   ★

By contrast, I spoke to a hundred people a week, but most of the communication was through e-mail or text. I was never without a BlackBerry. My conversations could be a few words. 'Call tomorrow.' Or 'C U There.' I kept things short.

The Reb didn't do short. He didn't do e-mail. 'In an e-mail, how can I tell if something is wrong?' he said. 'They can write anything. I want to see them. If not, I want to hear them. If I can't see them or hear them, how can I help them?'

He exhaled.

'Of course, in the old days . . . ,' he said.

Then suddenly, he was singing:

'In the olllld days . . . I would go door to dooor . . .'

I remember, as a child, when the Reb came to someone's house on our street. I remember pulling the curtain and looking out the window, maybe seeing his car parked out front. Of course, it was a different time. Doctors made house calls. Milkmen delivered to your stoop. No one had a security system.

The Reb would come to comfort a grieving family. He'd come if a child ran away or if someone got laid off. How nice would that be today if when a job was lost, a Man of God sat at the dinner table and encouraged you?

Instead, the idea seems almost archaic, if not invasive. No one wants to violate your 'space.'

Do you ever make house calls anymore? I asked.

'Only if asked,' the Reb replied.

Do you ever get a call from someone who isn't a member of your congregation?

'Certainly. In fact, two weeks ago, I got a call from the hospital. The person said, 'A dying woman has requested a rabbi.' So I went.

'When I got there, I saw a man sitting in a chair beside a woman who was gasping for breath. 'Who are you?' he said. 'Why are you here?'

'"I got a call," I said. 'They told me someone is dying and wants to speak to me.'

'He got angry. "Take a look at her," he said. "Can she talk? I didn't call you. *Who called you?*"

'I had no answer. So I let him rant. After a while, when he cooled down, he asked, "Are you married?" I said yes. He said, "Do you love your wife?" "Yes", I said. "Would you want to see her die?" "Not so long as there was hope for her to live," I said.

'We spoke for about an hour. At the end I said, "Do you mind if I recite a prayer for your wife?" He said he would appreciate that. So I did.'

And then? I asked.

'And then I left.'

I shook my head. He spent an hour talking to a stranger? I tried to remember the last time I'd done that. Or if I'd *ever* done that.

Did you ever find out who called you? I asked.

'Well, not officially. But, on my way out, I saw a nurse who I remembered from other visits. She was a devout Christian. When I saw her, our eyes met, and even though she didn't say anything, I knew it was her.'

Wait. A Christian woman called for a Jewish rabbi?

'She saw a man suffering. She didn't want him to be alone.'

She had a lot of guts.

'Yes,' he said. 'And a lot of love.'

A LITTLE MORE HISTORY

Albert Lewis may have reached the point where a Christian nurse would call him for help, but traversing religious prejudices had not always been so smooth. Remember when Moses referred to himself as a 'stranger in a strange land'? That phrase could have hung over the door when the Reb arrived in Haddon Heights, New Jersey, in 1948.

Back then, the borough was a railroad suburb, with trains running west to Philadelphia and east to the Atlantic Ocean. There were eight churches in town and just one synagogue – if you could call it that – a converted three-story Victorian house, with a Catholic church down one street and an Episcopalian church down another. While the churches had spires and brick facades, the Reb's 'temple' had a porch, a kitchen on the ground floor, bedrooms turned to classrooms, and old movie theater seats that had been installed for sanctuary use. A winding staircase ran up the middle.

The original 'congregation' was maybe three dozen families, some of whom drove forty minutes to get there. They had sent a letter to the seminary desperately seeking a rabbi; if none was available, they would have to close down, because it was a struggle to continue operating. Initially, some neighborhood Christians had signed a petition to keep the synagogue from forming. The idea of a Jewish 'community' was alien and threatening to them.

Once Al accepted the job, he set out to correct that. He joined the local ministerium. He reached out to clerics of all faiths. He tried to dispel any bad assumptions or prejudices by visiting schools and churches.

Some visits were easier than others.

One time, he was sitting in a church classroom, explaining his religion to the students. A boy raised his hand with a question.

'Where are your horns?'

The Reb was stunned.

'Where are your horns? Don't all Jews have horns?'

The Reb sighed and invited the boy to the front of the room. He removed the skullcap *(kippah)* that he wore on his head and asked the boy to run his hands through his hair.

'Do you feel any horns?'

The boy rubbed.

'Keep looking. Do you?'

The boy finally stopped.

'No,' he said, quietly.

'Ah.'

The boy sat down.

'Now where was I?' the Reb said.

Another time, the Reb invited an Episcopalian priest to address his congregation. The two men had become friendly, and the Reb thought it a good idea if clergymen were welcome in each other's sanctuaries.

It was a Friday night service. After prayers were sung, the priest was introduced. He stepped to the pulpit. The congregation quieted.

'It's a pleasure for me to be here,' he said, 'and I thank the rabbi for inviting me . . .'

Suddenly, tears began to well in his eyes. He spoke about how good a man Albert Lewis was. Then he blurted out, in a gush of emotion, 'That is why, please, you must help me get your rabbi to *accept Jesus Christ as his savior.*'

Dead silence.

'He's a lovely person,' the priest lamented, 'and *I don't want him to go to hell . . .*'

More dead silence.

'Please, *have him accept Jesus. Please . . .*'

Few attendees ever forgot *that* service.

And then there was the time when a member of the Reb's congregation, a German immigrant named Gunther Dreyfus, came racing in during a High Holiday service and pulled the Reb aside.

Gunther's face was ashen. His voice was shaking.

'What's wrong?' the Reb asked.

Apparently, minutes earlier, Gunther had been outside, overseeing the parking, when the Catholic priest came stomping out and began to yell about all the cars parking by his church, because it was a Sunday and he wanted the spaces for his members.

'Get them out of here,' he hollered, according to Gunther. 'You Jews move your cars now!'

'But it's the High Holiday,' Gunther said.

'Why must you have it on a Sunday?' the priest yelled.

'The date was set three thousand years ago,' Gunther replied. Being an immigrant, he still spoke with a German accent. The priest glared at him, then uttered something almost beyond belief.

'They didn't exterminate enough of you.'

Gunther was enraged. His wife had spent three and a half years in a concentration camp. He wanted to slug the priest. Someone intervened, thankfully, and a shaken Gunther returned to the sanctuary.

The next day, the Reb phoned the Catholic archbishop who oversaw the area's churches and told him what had happened. The following day, the phone rang. It was the priest, asking if he could come over and talk.

The Reb met him at the office door. They sat down.

'I want to apologize,' he said.

'Yes,' the Reb said.

'I should not have said what I did.'

'No, you should not have,' the Reb said.

'My archbishop had a suggestion,' the priest said.

'What is that?'

'Well, as you know, our Catholic school is in session now. And they will have their recess soon . . .'

The Reb listened.

Then he nodded and stood up.

And when the school doors opened and the kids burst out for recess, they saw the priest of St Rose of Lima Catholic Church and the rabbi of Temple Beth Sholom walking arm in arm, around the schoolyard.

Some kids blinked.

Some kids stared.

But all of them took notice.

You might think that an uneasy truce; two men forced to walk around a schoolyard, arm in arm. You might think a certain bitterness would haunt the relationship. But somehow, in time, they became friends. And years later, the Reb would be inside that Catholic church.

At the priest's funeral.

'I was asked to help officiate,' the Reb recalled. 'I recited a prayer for him. And I think, by that time, he might have thought it wasn't so bad.'

LIFE OF HENRY

Henry was often told 'Jesus loves you,' and it must have been true. Because he kept getting second chances.

While he was in prison, Henry boxed well enough to win a heavyweight competition, and he studied well enough to earn an associate's degree, even though he had never finished junior high.

When he got out of prison, he found a job in the exterminating business. He married his long-time girlfriend, Annette, and for a short while they lived a straight, normal life. Annette got pregnant. Henry hoped for a son.

Then one night, he came home and she was doubled over. They rushed to the hospital. The baby was born, three months premature, a tiny boy who barely weighed a pound. They named him Jerell. The doctors warned that his chances of survival were bleak, but Henry held the child in the palm of his big hand and he kissed the tiny feet.

'My son,' he whispered. Then he turned to God and asked for his help. 'Let him live. Please, let him live.'

Five days later, the baby died.

Henry and Annette buried their child in a cemetery on Long Island. For a while, Henry wondered if the Lord had punished him for the things he had done.

But soon he turned bitter. His business soured, his house went into foreclosure, and when he saw that his drug-dealing brother had more hundred-dollar bills than he had singles, Henry turned his back on God and second chances and returned to the business of breaking the law.

He began by dealing a small supply of drugs, then a larger amount, then a larger amount. The money came in fast. Soon, he was acting like a kingpin, glorifying himself, giving orders. He bought fancy clothes. He styled his hair. He actually made people kneel down when they wanted something. Only when mothers came with babies did he soften up. They would offer him anything in exchange for drugs: groceries they'd just purchased, sometimes even a baby girl's tiny earring.

'Keep it,' he would say, giving them a small bag. 'But that earring belongs to me now. I want to see it on that baby every time you come in here.'

At one point, in the mid-1980s, Henry was making tens of thousands of dollars per month. He sold drugs at fancy parties, often to 'respectable' types like judges, lawyers, even an off-duty cop. Henry smirked at their weakness and his momentary power.

But one night, he made a common and fatal error: he decided to try some of his own product.

That was the cliff. And off it he flew.

Soon Henry was addicted to his own poison, and he wanted only to lose himself in a cloud of crack cocaine. Often he used the very product he was supposed to sell, and then, to cover up, he'd invent outlandish excuses.

Like the time he took a cigarette and burned holes into his arm, so he could tell his dealers he'd been tortured and the drugs stolen.

Or the time he had a friend shoot him in the leg with a .25 automatic, so he could tell his dealers he'd been robbed. They still came to the hospital, demanding to see the wound.

One bad night, already high and needing more money, he and a few others, including a nephew and a brother-in-law, drove a Coupe DeVille out to Canarsie, Brooklyn. Their method of assault was to pull the car alongside an unsuspecting target, jump out, demand the money, and ride off.

This time, it was an elderly couple. Henry sprang from the car and waved a gun in their faces.

'You know what this is!' he yelled.

The old woman screamed.

'Shut up or I'll blow your head off,' he screamed back.

The couple surrendered their money, jewelry, and watches. Henry was unsettled by their older faces. A pang of conscience hit him. But it didn't stop him. Soon the Coupe DeVille was racing away down Flatland Avenue.

And then a siren sounded. Lights flashed. Henry shouted at his nephew to keep driving. He rolled down the windows and out it all went. The jewelry. The money. Even their guns.

Moments later, the police overtook them.

At the station, Henry was put in a lineup. He waited. Then the officers brought in the elderly man.

And Henry knew he was sunk.

Once the man identified him, Henry would be charged, convicted, and face fifteen years in prison. Life as he knew it would be over. Why had he risked it all? He had literally thrown everything out the window.

'Is that him?' the officer asked.

Henry swallowed.

'I can't be sure,' the old man mumbled.

What?

'Look again,' the officer said.

'I can't be sure,' the old man said.

Henry could not believe his ears. How could the man not finger him? He had waved a gun *right in his face*.

But because the ID was not certain, Henry was let go. He went home. He lay down. He told himself the Lord had done that. The Lord was being merciful. The Lord was giving him another chance. And the Lord did not want him stealing anymore, using drugs anymore, or terrorizing people anymore.

And perhaps it was true.

But he still did not listen.

IT IS 1974 . . .

. . . and I am in my religious high school. The subject is the parting of the Red Sea. I yawn. What is left to learn about this? I've heard it a million times. I look across the room to a girl I like and contemplate how hard it would be to get her attention.

'There is a Talmudic commentary here,' the teacher says.

Oh, great, *I figure. This means translation, which is slow and painful. But as the story unfolds, I begin to pay attention.*

After the Israelites safely crossed the Red Sea, the Egyptians chased after them and were drowned. God's angels wanted to celebrate the enemy's demise.

According to the commentary, God saw this and grew angry. He said, in essence: 'Stop celebrating. For those were my children, too.'

Those were my children, too.

'What do you think of that?' the teacher asks us.

Someone else answers. But I know what I think. I think it is the first time I've heard that God might love the 'enemy' as well as us.

Years later, I will forget the class, forget the teacher's name, forget the girl across the room. But I will remember that story.

JULY

THE GREATEST QUESTION OF ALL

I n any conversation, I was taught, there are at least three parties: you, the other person, and the Lord.

I recalled that lesson on a summer day in the small office when both the Reb and I wore shorts. My bare leg stuck with perspiration to the green leather chair, and I raised it with a small *thwock*.

The Reb was looking for a letter. He lifted a pad, then an envelope, then a newspaper. I knew he'd never find it. I think the mess in his office was almost a way of life now, a game that kept the world interesting. As I waited, I glanced at the file on the lower shelf, the one marked 'God.' We still hadn't opened it.

'Ach,' he said, giving up.

Can I ask you something?

'Ask away, young scholar,' he crowed.

How do you know God exists?

He stopped. A smile crept across his face.

'An excellent question.'

He pressed his fingers into his chin.

And the answer? I said.

'First, make the case against Him.'

Okay, I said, taking his challenge. How about this? We live in a world where your genes can be mapped, where your cells can be copied, where your face can be altered. Heck, with surgery, you can go from being a man to being a woman. We have science to tell us of the earth's creation; rocket probes explore the universe. The sun is no longer a mystery. And the moon – which people used to worship? We brought some of it home in a pouch, right?

'Go on,' he said.

So why, in such a place, where the once-great mysteries have been solved, does anyone still believe in God or Jesus or Allah or a Supreme Being of any kind? Haven't we outgrown it? Isn't it like Pinocchio, the puppet? When he found he could move without his strings, did he still look the same way at Geppetto?

The Reb tapped his fingers together.

'That's some speech.'

You said make a case.

'Ah.'

He leaned in. 'Now. My turn. Look, if you say that science will eventually prove there is no God, on that I must differ. No matter how small they take it back, to a tadpole, to an atom, there is always something they can't explain, something that created it all at the end of the search.

'And no matter how far they try to go the other way – to extend life, play around with the genes, clone this, clone that, live to one hundred and fifty – at some point, life is over. And then what happens? When life comes to an end?'

I shrugged.

'You see?'

He leaned back. He smiled.

'When you come to the end, that's where God begins.'

Many great minds have set out to disprove God's existence. Sometimes, they retreat to the opposite view. C. S. Lewis, who wrote so eloquently of faith, initially wrestled with the very concept of God and called himself 'the most dejected and reluctant convert in all of England.' Louis Pasteur, the great scientist, tried to disprove a divine existence through facts and research; in the end, the grand design of man convinced him otherwise.

A spate of recent books had declared God a fool's notion, hocus-pocus, a panacea for weak minds. I thought the Reb would find these offensive, but he never did. He understood that the journey to belief was not straight, easy, or even always logical. He respected an educated argument, even if he didn't agree with it.

Personally, I always wondered about authors and celebrities who loudly declared there was no God. It was usually when they were healthy and popular and being listened to by crowds. What happens, I wondered, in the quiet moments before death? By then, they have lost the stage, the world has moved on. If suddenly, in their last gasping moments, through fear, a vision, a late enlightenment, they change their minds about God, who would know?

The Reb was a believer from the start, that was clear, but I also knew that he was not crazy about some things God allowed on this earth. He had lost a daughter, many years ago. That had shaken his world. And he regularly cried after visiting once-robust members of the congregation who now lay helpless in hospital beds.

'Why so much pain?' he would say, looking to the heavens. 'Take them already. What is the point?'

I once asked the Reb that most common of faith questions: why do bad things happen to good people? It had been answered countless times in countless ways; in books, in sermons, on Web sites, in tear-filled hugs. *The Lord wanted her with him . . . He died doing what he loved . . . She was a gift . . . This is a test . . .*

I remember a family friend whose son was struck with a terrible medical affliction. After that, at any religious ceremony – even a wedding – I would see the man out in the hallway, refusing to enter the service. 'I just can't listen to it anymore,' he would say. His faith had been lost.

When I asked the Reb, Why do bad things happen to good people?, he gave none of the standard answers. He quietly said, 'No one knows.' I admired that. But when I asked if that ever shook his belief in God, he was firm.

'I cannot waver,' he said.

Well, you could, if you didn't believe in something all-powerful.

'An atheist,' he said.

Yes.

'And then I could explain why my prayers were not answered.'

Right.

He studied me carefully. He drew in his breath.

'I had a doctor once who was an atheist. Did I ever tell you about him?'

No.

'This doctor, he liked to jab me and my beliefs. He used to schedule my appointments deliberately on Saturdays, so I would have to call the receptionist and explain why, because of my religion, that wouldn't work.'

Nice guy, I said.

'Anyhow, one day, I read in the paper that his brother had died. So I made a condolence call.'

After the way he treated you?

'In this job,' the Reb said, 'you don't retaliate.'

I laughed.

'So I go to his house, and he sees me. I can tell he is upset. I tell him I am sorry for his loss. And he says, with an angry face, 'I envy you.'

'"Why do you envy me?" I said.

'"Because when you lose someone you love, you can curse God. You can yell. You can blame him.

87

You can demand to know why. But I don't believe in God. I'm a *doctor*! And I couldn't help my brother!"

'He was near tears. "Who do I blame?" he kept asking me. "There is no God. I can only blame myself."'

The Reb's face tightened, as if in pain.

'That,' he said, softly, 'is a terrible self-indictment.'

Worse than an unanswered prayer?

'Oh yes. It is far more comforting to think God listened and said no, than to think that nobody's out there.'

LIFE OF HENRY

He was now approaching his thirtieth birthday, a criminal, an addict, and a liar to the Lord. He had a wife. It didn't stop him. He had a daughter. It didn't stop him. His money was gone, his fancy clothes were gone, his hair was unstyled and coarse. It didn't stop him.

One Saturday night, he wanted so desperately to get high that he drove with two men to Jamaica, Queens, to the only people he could think of with both money and product – drug dealers he used to work for.

He knocked on their door. They answered.

He pulled a gun.

'What are you doing?' they said, incredulous.

'You know what this is,' he said.

The gun didn't even have a firing pin in it. Luckily, the dealers didn't know that. Henry waved it and barked, 'Let's go,' and they gave him their money and their jewelry and their drugs.

He drove off with his friends, even gave them the valuables, but he kept the poison for himself. It was all his body wanted. It was all he could think about.

Later that night, after he'd smoked and sniffed and guzzled alcohol as well, paranoia set in, and Henry realized the dumb mistake he had made. His victims knew who he was and where he lived. And they would want revenge.

Which is when Henry grabbed that shotgun, went out front, and hid behind a row of trash cans. His wife was confused and scared.

'What's happening?' she said, crying.

'Shut the lights!' he yelled.

He saw his daughter, watching from the doorway.

'Stay inside!'

He waited. He trembled. Something told him that for all the trouble he had escaped, this would be the night it caught up with him. A car would come down his block, and he would die from a spray of bullets.

And so, one last time, he turned to God.

'Will you save me, Jesus?' he whispered. 'If I promise to give myself to you, will you save me tonight?' He was weeping. He was breathing heavily. If, with all the wrong he'd done, he was still allowed to pray, then this was as close as he came to true prayer. 'Hear me, Jesus, please . . .'

He had been a troubled child.

A delinquent teen.

A bad man.

Could he still be a saved soul?

The only tyrant I accept in this world is the still voice within.

MOHANDAS GANDHI

AUGUST

WHY WAR?

The summer moved quickly. The war in Iraq dominated the headlines, as did a battle to put the Ten Commandments in front of an Alabama courthouse. I found myself phoning the Reb in between visits. His voice was always upbeat.

'Is this Detroit calling?' he might begin.

Or: 'Rabbi hotline, how can I help you?'

It made me ashamed of the way I sometimes answered the phone (a rushed 'Hello?' as if it was a question I didn't want to ask). In all the time I knew the Reb, I don't think I ever heard him say, 'Lemme call you back.' I marveled at how a man who was supposed to be available for so many people could somehow be available for each one of them.

On a late August visit, the Reb's wife, Sarah, a kind and eloquent woman who'd been with him for sixty years, answered the door and led me to his office. The Reb was already seated, wearing a long-sleeved shirt despite the summer heat. His downy white hair was neatly combed, but I noticed that he didn't get up. He just stretched out his arms for a hug.

Are you okay? I said.

He flung his palms in opposite directions.

'Lemme put it this way. I'm not as good as I was yesterday, buuuut . . . I'm better than I'm gonna be tom-orr-rrr-ow . . .'

You and singing, I said.

'Ah,' he laughed. 'I sing a song, you hum along . . .'

I sat down.

A newspaper was open on his desk. The Reb kept up with the news, as much as he could. When I asked how long he thought the Iraq war would last, he shrugged.

You've lived through a lot of wars, I said.

'Yes.'

Do they ever make more sense?

'No.'

This one, we agreed, was particularly troubling. Suicide bombings. Hidden explosives. It's not like the old wars, I said, with tanks coming one way, tanks coming the other.

'But, Mitch, even in this new age of horror,' the Reb noted, 'you can find small acts of human kindness. Something I saw a few years ago, on a trip to Israel to visit my daughter, stays with me to this day.

'I was sitting on a balcony. I heard a blast. I turned around and saw smoke coming from a shopping area. It was one of these terrible . . . uh . . . whachacalls . . .'

Bombs? Car bombs?

'That's it,' he said. 'I went from the apartment, as fast as I could, and as I arrived, a car pulled up in front of me. And a young fellow jumps out. He is wearing a yellow vest, so I follow him.

'When I get to the scene, I see the car that has been blown up. A woman was apparently doing laundry; she was one of the people killed.

'And there, in the street . . .' He swallowed. 'There . . . in the street . . . were people picking up her body pieces. Carefully. Collecting anything. A hand. A finger.'

He looked down.

'They were wearing gloves, and moving very deliberately, a piece of a leg here, skin there, even the blood. You know why? They were following religious law, which says all pieces of the body must be buried together. They were putting life over death, even in the face of this . . . atrocity . . . because life is what God gives us, and how can you just let a piece of God's gift lie there in the street?'

I had heard of this group, called ZAKA – yellow-vested volunteers who want to ensure that the deceased are treated with dignity. They arrive at these scenes sometimes faster than the paramedics.

'I cried when I saw that,' the Reb said. 'I just cried. The kindness that takes. The belief. Picking up pieces of your dead. This is who we are. This beautiful faith.'

We sat quietly for a minute.

Why does man kill man? I finally asked.

He touched his forefingers to his lips. Then he pushed in his chair and rolled slowly to a stack of books.

'Let me find something here . . .'

Albert Lewis was born during World War I. He was a seminary student during World War II. His congregation was peppered with veterans and Holocaust survivors, some who still bore tattooed numbers on their wrists.

Over the years, he watched young congregants depart for the Korean War and the Vietnam War. His son-in-law and grandchildren served in the Israeli Army. So war was never far from his mind. Nor were its consequences.

Once, on a trip to Israel after the war in 1967, he went with a group to an area on the northern border and found himself wandering through some abandoned buildings. There, in the ruins of one destroyed house, he discovered an Arabic schoolbook lying in the dirt. It was facedown, missing a cover.

He brought it home.

Now he held it on his lap. This was what he'd gone looking for. A schoolbook nearly forty years old.

'Here.' He handed it over. 'Look through it.'

It was fraying. Its binding had shriveled. The back page, torn and curled, had a cartoon image of a schoolgirl, a cat, and a rabbit, which had been colored in with crayon. The book was obviously for young kids and the whole thing was in Arabic, so I couldn't understand a word.

Why did you keep this? I asked.

'Because I wanted to be reminded of what had happened there. The buildings were empty. The people were gone.

'I felt I had to save something.'

Most religions warn against war, yet more wars have been fought over religion than perhaps anything else. Christians have killed Jews, Jews have killed Muslims, Muslims have killed Hindus, Hindus have killed Buddhists, Catholics have killed Protestants, Orthodox have killed pagans, and you could run that list backward and sideways and it would still be true. War never stops; it only pauses.

I asked the Reb if, over the years, he had changed his view about war and violence.

'Do you remember Sodom and Gomorrah?' he asked.

Yes. That one I remember.

'So you know Abraham realized those people were bad. He knew they were miserable, vicious. But what does he do? He argues with God against destroying the cities. He says, Can you at least spare them if there are fifty good people there? God says okay. Then he goes down to forty, then thirty. He knows there aren't that many. He bargains all the way down to ten before he closes the deal.'

And they still fell short, I said.

'And they still fell short,' the Reb confirmed. 'But you see? Abraham's instinct was correct. You must first argue *against* warfare, against violence and destruction, because these are not normal ways of living.'

But so many people wage wars in God's name.

'Mitch,' the Reb said, 'God does not want such killing to go on.'

Then why hasn't it stopped?

He lifted his eyebrows.

'Because man does.'

He was right, of course. You can sense man's drumbeat to war. Vengeance rises. Tolerance is mocked. Over the years, I was taught why our side was right. And in another country someone my age was taught the opposite.

'There's a reason I gave that book to you,' the Reb said.

What's the reason?

'Open it.'

I opened it.

'More.'

I flipped through the pages and out fell three small black-and-white photos, faded and smudged with dirt.

One was of an older dark-haired woman, Arabic and matronly looking. One was of a mustached younger Arabic man in a suit and tie. The last photo was of two children, side by side, presumably a brother and sister.

Who are they? I asked.

'I don't know,' he said, softly.

He held out his hand and I gave him the photo of the children.

'Over the years, I kept seeing these kids, the mother, her son. That's why I never threw the book away. I felt I had to keep them alive somehow.

'I thought maybe someday someone would look at the pictures, say they knew the family, and return them to the survivors. But I'm running out of time.'

He handed me the photo back.

Wait, I said. I don't understand. From your religious viewpoint, these people were the enemy.

His voice grew angry.

'Enemy schmenemy,' he said. 'This was a *family*.'

FROM A SERMON BY THE REB, 1975

'A man seeks employment on a farm. He hands his letter of recommendation to his new employer. It reads simply, "He sleeps in a storm."

'The owner is desperate for help, so he hires the man.

'Several weeks pass, and suddenly, in the middle of the night, a powerful storm rips through the valley.

'Awakened by the swirling rain and howling wind, the owner leaps out of bed. He calls for his new hired hand, but the man is sleeping soundly.

'So he dashes off to the barn. He sees, to his amazement, that the animals are secure with plenty of feed.

'He runs out to the field. He sees the bales of wheat have been bound and are wrapped in tarpaulins.

'He races to the silo. The doors are latched, and the grain is dry.

'And then he understands. "He sleeps in a storm."

'My friends, if we tend to the things that are

important in life, if we are right with those we love and behave in line with our faith, our lives will not be cursed with the aching throb of unfulfilled business. Our words will always be sincere, our embraces will be tight. We will never wallow in the agony of "I could have, I should have." We can sleep in a storm.

'And when it's time, our good-byes will be complete.'

LIFE OF HENRY

Henry Covington did not sleep that night. But he did not die, either.

The drug dealers from whom he'd stolen somehow never found him; the cars that came down his street did not fire a bullet. He hid behind those trash cans, gripping his shotgun and reciting his question over and over.

'Will you save me, Jesus?'

He was following man's sad tradition of running to God when all else fails. He had done it before, turned his face to the heavens, only to return to new trouble when the current trouble passed.

But this time, when the sun rose, Henry Covington slid the shotgun under his bed and lay down next to his wife and child.

It was Easter Sunday.

Henry thought about his life. He had stolen and lied and waved guns in people's faces. He had blown all his money on drugs, and he had been so low at one point he had a small pebble of crack cocaine but nothing to smoke it in, so he scoured the streets until he found a cigarette butt. Anyone could have stepped on that cigarette butt. A dog could have urinated on it. It didn't matter. He put it in his mouth. He had to have what he had to have.

Now, on Easter morning, he suddenly had to have something else. It was hard to explain. Even his wife didn't understand it. An acquaintance came by with heroin. Henry's eyes desired it. His body craved it. But if he took it, it would kill him. He knew it. He was certain. He had promised his life to God in the darkness behind those trash cans, and here, hours later, was his first test.

He told the man to go away.

Then Henry went into the bathroom, got on his knees, and began to pray. After he finished, he guzzled a bottle of NyQuil.

The next day, he guzzled another.

And the next day, he guzzled another – all in an attempt to numb himself through a self-imposed detox. It was three days before he could put a morsel of food in his mouth. Three days before he could even lift up out of bed.

Three days.

And then he opened his eyes.

SEPTEMBER

HAPPINESS

The Reb opened his eyes.

He was in the hospital.

It was not the first time. Although he often hid his ailments from me, I learned that in recent months, staying upright had become a problem. He had slipped on the pavement and cut open his forehead. He had slipped in the house and banged his neck and cheek. Now he had fallen getting up from his chair and slammed his rib cage against a desk. It was either syncope, a temporary loss of consciousness, or small strokes, transient attacks that left him dizzy and disoriented.

Either way, it was not good.

Now I expected the worst. A hospital. The portal to the end. I had called and asked if it was all right to visit, and Sarah kindly said I could come.

I braced myself at the front entrance. I am haunted by hospital visits and their familiar, depressing cues. The antiseptic smell. The low drone of TV sets. The drawn curtains. The occasional moaning from another bed. I had been to too many hospitals for too many people.

For the first time in a while, I thought about our agreement.

Will you do my eulogy?

I entered the Reb's room.

'Ah,' he smiled, looking up from the bed, 'a visitor from afar . . .'

I stopped thinking about it.

We hugged – or, I should say, I hugged his shoulders and he touched my head – and we both agreed that this was a first, a hospital conversation. His robe fell open slightly and I caught a glance at his bare chest, soft, loose flesh with a few silver hairs. I felt a rush of shame and looked away.

A nurse breezed in.

'How are you doing today?' she asked.

'I'm dooooing,' the Reb lilted. 'I'm dooooing . . .'

She laughed. 'He sings all the time, this one.'

Yes, he does, I said.

It amazed me how consistently the Reb could summon his good nature. To sing to the nurses. To kid around with the physicians. The previous day, while waiting in a wheelchair in the hallway, he was asked by a hospital worker for a blessing. So the Reb put his hands on the man's head and gave him one.

He refused to wallow in self-pity. In fact, the worse things got for him, the more intent he seemed on making sure no one around him was saddened by it.

As we sat in the room, a commercial for an anti-depressant drug flashed across the TV screen. It showed people looking forlorn, alone on a bench or staring out a window.

'*I keep feeling something bad is going to happen . . . ,*' the TV voice said.

Then, after showing the pill and some graphics, those same people appeared again, looking happier.

The Reb and I watched in silence. After it ended, he asked, 'Do you think those pills work?'

Not like that, I said.

'No,' he agreed. 'Not like that.'

Happiness in a tablet. This is our world. Prozac. Paxil. Xanax. Billions are spent to advertise such drugs. And billions more are spent purchasing them. You don't even need a specific trauma; just 'general depression' or 'anxiety,' as if sadness were as treatable as the common cold.

I knew depression was real, and in many cases required medical attention. I also knew we overused the word. Much of what we called 'depression' was really dissatisfaction, a result of setting a bar impossibly high or expecting treasures that we weren't willing to work for. I knew people whose unbearable source of misery was their weight, their baldness, their lack of advancement in a workplace, or their inability to find the perfect mate, even if they themselves did not behave like one. To these people, unhappiness was a condition, an intolerable state of affairs. If pills could help, pills were taken.

105

But pills were not going to change the fundamental problem in the construction. Wanting what you can't have. Looking for self-worth in the mirror. Layering work on top of work and still wondering why you weren't satisfied – before working some more.

I knew. I had done all that. There was a stretch where I could not have worked more hours in the day without eliminating sleep altogether. I piled on accomplishments. I made money. I earned accolades. And the longer I went at it, the emptier I began to feel, like pumping air faster and faster into a torn tire.

The time I spent with Morrie, my old professor, had tapped my brakes on much of that. After watching him die, and seeing what mattered to him at the end, I cut back. I limited my schedule.

But I still kept my hands on my own wheel. I didn't turn things over to fate or faith. I recoiled from people who put their daily affairs in divine hands, saying, 'If God wants it, it will happen.' I kept silent when people said all that mattered was their personal relationship with Jesus. Such surrender seemed silly to me. I felt like I knew better. But privately, I couldn't say I felt any happier than they did.

So I noted how, for all the milligrams of medication he required, the Reb never popped a pill for his peace of mind. He loved to smile. He avoided anger. He was never haunted by 'Why am I here?' He knew why he was here, he said: to give to others, to celebrate God, and to enjoy and honor the world he was put in. His morning prayers began with 'Thank you, Lord, for returning my soul to me.'

When you start that way, the rest of the day is a bonus.

Can I ask you something?

'Yes,' he said.

What makes a man happy?

'Well . . .' He rolled his eyes around the hospital room. 'This may not be the best setting for that question.'

Yeah, you're right.

'On the other hand . . .' He took a deep breath. 'On the other hand, here in this building, we must face the real issues. Some people will get better. Some will not. So it may be a good place to define what that word means.'

Happiness?

'That's right. The things society tells us we must have to be happy – a new this or that, a bigger house, a better job. I know the falsity of it. I have counseled many people who have all these things, and I can tell you they are not happy because of them.

'The number of marriages that have disintegrated when they had all the stuff in the world. The families who fought and argued all the time, when they had money and health. Having more does not keep you from wanting more. And if you always want more – to be richer, more beautiful, more well known – you are missing the bigger picture, and I can tell you from experience, happiness will never come.'

You're not going to tell me to stop and smell the roses, are you?

He chuckled. 'Roses would smell better than this place.'

Suddenly, out in the hall, I heard an infant scream, followed by a quick 'shhh!' presumably from its mother. The Reb heard it, too.

'Now, that child,' he said, 'reminds me of something our sages taught. When a baby comes into the world, its hands are clenched, right? Like this?'

He made a fist.

'Why? Because a baby, not knowing any better, wants to grab everything, to say, 'The whole world is mine.'

'But when an old person dies, how does he do so? With his hands open. Why? Because he has learned the lesson.'

What lesson? I asked.

He stretched open his empty fingers.

'We can take nothing with us.'

For a moment we both stared at his hand. It was trembling.

'Ach, you see this?' he said.

Yeah.

'I can't make it stop.'

He dropped the hand to his chest. I heard a cart being wheeled down the hall. He spoke so wisely, with such passion, that for a moment I'd forgotten where we were.

'Anyhow,' he said, his voice trailing off.

I hated seeing him in that bed. I wanted him home, with the messy desk and the mismatched clothes. I forced a smile.

So, have we solved the secret of happiness?

'I believe so,' he said.

Are you going to tell me?

'Yes. Ready?'

Ready.

'Be satisfied.'

That's it?

'Be grateful.'

That's it?

'For what you have. For the love you receive. And for what God has given you.'

That's it?

He looked me in the eye. Then he sighed deeply. 'That's it.'

THE END OF SUMMER

When I left the hospital that day, I got a phone call from the Reb's youngest daughter, Gilah. She was about my age; I had known her during our school years, and we'd kept up loosely. She was funny, warm, opinionated, and deeply loving to her father.

'So, did he tell you?' she said, glumly.

What?

'The tumor.'

What?

'It's in his lung.'

Cancer?

'He didn't say anything?'

I looked at the phone.

He'd never said a word.

AUTUMN

CHURCH

In downtown Detroit, there is a church on Trumbull Avenue, across from an empty field. It is a huge, Gothic structure made of red brick and limestone, and it looks as if it blew in from another century. Pointy spires. Arched doorways. Stained glass windows, including one in which the apostle Paul asks, 'What must I do to be saved?'

The building itself dates back to 1881, when the neighborhood was full of mansions and wealthy Presbyterians. They built the church to hold twelve hundred members, the largest such congregation in the Midwest. Now the mansions are gone, so are the Presbyterians, and in this poor, barren neighborhood, the church seems forgotten. The walls are decaying. The roof is crumbling. Over the years, some of the stained glass panels were stolen, and some windows have been boarded up.

I used to drive past this church on my way to Tiger Stadium, a famous baseball park a half mile down the street. I never went inside. I never saw anyone go inside.

For all I knew, the place was abandoned.

I was about to find out.

In the months since the Reb had surprised me with those words *enemy schmenemy*, I had been forced to rethink some of my own prejudices. The truth was, while I tried to be a charitable man, I still drew mental lines between 'my' side and the 'other' side – whether cultural, ethnic, or religious. I had been taught, as many of us are, that charity begins at home, and helping your own kind should come first.

But who *was* my 'own kind'? I lived far from where I was raised. I married a woman from a different faith. I was a white man in an overwhelmingly African-American city. And while I had been lucky financially, Detroit was going broke around me. The near-depression that would soon hit the nation foretold itself in our streets. Jobs disappeared at an alarming rate. Homes were foreclosed. Buildings were abandoned. Our daily bread, the auto industry, was crumbling, and the swelling numbers of unemployed and homeless were scary.

One night I found myself at a downtown shelter, a Christian rescue mission, where I decided to spend the night and write about the experience. I waited on line for a blanket and soap. I was given a bed. I heard a minister preach about Jesus and was surprised at how many of the weary men, chins in their hands, still listened to how they could be saved.

At one point, in line for food, a man turned and asked if I was who he thought I was.

Yes, I said.

He nodded slowly.

'So . . . What happened to you?'

That night motivated me to create a charity for the homeless. We raised and distributed money to area shelters. We took pride in no overhead or administrative fees, and if we couldn't see and touch where the disbursements went, we didn't proceed. That meant many in-person visits.

And so, on a humid September afternoon, I pulled my car up to the old, decaying church on Trumbull. The pastor, I had been told, ran a small shelter there. I had come to see if it needed assistance.

A traffic signal swayed in the wind. I stepped from the car and clicked the lock button on my key. A man and a woman, both African-American, were sitting by the church wall in fold-up aluminum chairs, the cheap kind we used to take to the beach. They stared at me. The man was missing his left leg.

I'm looking for the pastor, I said.

The woman rose. She pushed through a small red door that was weakly hinged. I waited. The one-legged man, his crutches resting against the chair, smiled at me. He wore glasses and was missing most of his front teeth.

'Kinda warm today,' he said.

Yeah, I said.

I glanced at my watch. I shifted on my feet. Finally, I saw movement in the shadows.

And then.

And then out stepped a large man.

An *extremely* large man.

He was, I would learn, fifty years old – although his face was still boyish, with a thin, close-cropped beard – and he was tall as a basketball player, but he had to weigh more than four hundred pounds. His body seemed to unroll in layers, a broad slab of a chest cascading into a huge belly that hung like a pillow over the belt of his pants. His arms spread the sleeves of his oversized white T-shirt. His forehead was sweating, and he breathed heavily, as if he'd just climbed stairs.

If this is a Man of God, I thought, *I'm the man in the moon.*

'Hello,' he rasped, holding out his hand. 'I'm Henry.'

FROM A SERMON BY THE REB, 1981

'A military chaplain' told me the following story:

'A soldier's little girl, whose father was being moved to a distant post, was sitting at the airport among her family's meager belongings.

'The girl was sleepy. She leaned against the packs and duffel bags.

'A lady came by, stopped, and patted her on the head.

'"Poor child," she said. "You haven't got a home."

'The child looked up in surprise.

'"But we *do* have a home," she said. "We just don't have a house to put it in."'

SEPTEMBER

WHAT IS RICH?

The Reb was using a walker now. I heard it thumping toward me as I stood outside his front door. It was September, three years after the hospital visit. The leaves were starting to change color, and I noticed a strange car in his driveway. His muffled voice sang from inside, 'I'm coming . . . hold on . . . *I'm coming . . .*'

The door opened. He smiled. He was thinner now than when I first began visiting; his arms were bonier and his face more drawn. His hair was white, and his once-tall body was bent at an angle. His fingers gripped the walker tightly.

'Say hello to my new companion,' he said, rattling the handles. 'We go everywhere together.'

He lowered his voice.

'I can't *shake* him!'

I laughed.

'So. Come.'

I stepped in behind him, as I always did, and he pushed, lifted and thumped his way to the office with all his books and the file on God.

★   ★   ★

The car belonged to a home health care worker who now came to the house to aid the Reb. It was an admission that his body could betray him without warning, an admission that things *could happen*. The tumor in his lung was still there. But at the Reb's advanced age – now eighty-nine – the doctors felt it was not worth the risk to remove it. Ironically, as the Reb slowed down, so did the aggressiveness of the cancer, like two tired combatants plodding toward a finish line.

Politely put, the doctors said, age would likely claim the Reb before any tumor did.

As we dragged down the hall, I realized another reason that car stood out: there was pretty much nothing new in this house since I started visiting six years earlier. The furniture hadn't changed. No carpet had been redone. The television had not grown in size.

The Reb had never been big on stuff.

But then, he'd never had much of it.

He was born in 1917, and his parents were poor even by the day's modest standards. Albert's mother was a Lithuanian immigrant, and his father, a textile salesman, was always in and out of work. They lived in a cramped apartment building on Topping Avenue in the Bronx. Food was scarce. Young Albert would come home from school each day praying not to see the family's furniture out in the street.

As the oldest of three – a sister and a brother followed him – he spent from sunrise to sunset in a religious academy called a yeshiva. He had no bicycles or fancy toys. Sometimes his mother would buy bread from the two-day-old bin, spread jam on it, and feed it to him with hot tea. He recalled that as 'the most heavenly meal of my childhood.'

As the Great Depression widened, Albert had but two sets of clothes, one for weekdays, one for Sabbath. His shoes were old and cobbled, his socks were washed out nightly. On the occasion of his Bar Mitzvah – the day, in his religion, that he became a man – his father gave him a new suit. He wore it as proudly as any kid could wear anything.

A few weeks later, wearing that same suit, he and his father took a trolley car to a relative's house, a well-to-do attorney. His father carried a cake that his mother had baked.

At the house, a teenage cousin came running up, took one look at Albert, and burst out laughing. 'Al, that's my old suit!' he squealed. 'Hey, guys! Look! Al's wearing my old suit!'

Albert was mortified. For the rest of the visit, he sat red-faced in humiliation. On the trolley ride home, he fought tears as he glared at his father, who had traded the cake for a suitcase full of clothes, an exchange the son now understood as rich relatives giving to poor ones.

Finally, when they got home, he couldn't hold it in any longer. 'I don't understand,' Albert burst out to his father. 'You're a religious man. Your cousin isn't. You pray every day. He doesn't. They have everything they want. And we have nothing!

His father nodded, then answered in Yiddish, in a slight singsong voice.

God and the decision he renders is correct.
God doesn't punish anyone out of the blue.
God knows what he is doing.

That was the last they spoke of it.

And the last time Albert Lewis judged life by what he owned.

Now, seventy-six years later, what he owned meant so little, it was a source of comedy. He dressed like a rummage sale. He mixed plaid shirts and loud socks with pants from Haband, a low-cost clothing line that featured items like polyester jeans and eleven-pocket vests. The Reb loved those things, the more pockets the better. He would stash notes, pens, tiny flashlights, five-dollar bills, clippings, pencils.

He was like a kid when it came to possessions; price tags meant nothing, small enjoyment meant everything. High tech? He liked a clock radio playing classical music. Fancy restaurants? His culinary pleasures were graham crackers and peanut butter cookies. His idea of a great meal was pouring cereal into his oatmeal, adding a cup of raisins, and stirring it all up. He adored food shopping, but only for bargains – a leftover habit from his Depression days – and his supermarket journeys were something of legend. He would push a cart through the aisles for hours, judiciously choosing the correct merchandise. Then, at the cash register, he would dole out coupon after coupon, joking with the cashiers, proudly adding up the savings.

For years, his wife had to pick up his paychecks, or else he'd never bother. His starting salary at the temple was just a few thousand dollars a year, and after five decades of service, his compensation was embarrassing compared to other clerics. He never pushed for more. He thought it unseemly. He didn't even own a car for the first few years of his service; a neighbor named Eddie Adelman would drive him into Philadelphia and drop him off at a subway so that he could take a class at Dropsie College.

The Reb seemed to embody a magnetic repulsion between faith and wealth. If congregants tried to give him things for free, he suggested they contribute to charity instead. He hated to fundraise, because he never felt a clergyman should ask people for money. He once said in a sermon that the only time he ever wished he was a millionaire was when he thought about how many families he could save from financial sorrow.

What he liked was old things. Old coins. Old paintings. Even his personal prayer book was old and fraying, stuffed with clippings and held together with rubber bands.

'I have what I need,' he said, surveying his messy shelves. 'Why bother chasing more?'

You're like that Biblical quote, I said. What profits a man if he gains the whole world, but loses his soul?

'That's Jesus.'

Oops, sorry, I said.

'Don't apologize,' he said, smiling. 'It's still good.'

CHURCH

As the Detroit traffic whizzed by outside, I walked through an oversized sanctuary with Pastor Henry Covington of the I Am My Brother's Keeper Ministry. It was a spectacular old room, with massive high ceilings, a large mahogany pulpit, a towering pipe organ, and an upper balcony of pews.

It was also rotting away.

Paint peeled everywhere. The plaster was cracking. Floorboards had deteriorated, and the carpet had dips that could twist your ankle. I looked up and saw a hole in the ceiling.

A huge hole.

Maybe ten feet long.

'That's a big problem,' Henry admitted. 'Especially when it rains.'

I noticed red buckets in strategic spots to catch the water. The white plaster was stained brown by seepage. I had never seen such a hole in a religious building. It looked like the hull of a ship blown apart by a cannon shot.

We sat down. Henry's belly hung so large in front of him, he seemed to hook his elbows over the pew for balance.

'I'm not sure why you're here,' he said politely.
You take care of homeless people, right?
'Yes, a couple of nights a week,' Henry said.
They eat here?
'Yes, in our gym.'
And sleep here?
'Yes.'
Do they have to be Christian?
'No.'
Do you try to convert them?
'No. We offer prayers. We ask if anyone wants to give their life to Jesus, but no one is forced. Anyone can come.'

I nodded. I told him about the charity. How maybe we could help.

'Oh.' His eyebrows lifted. 'Well. That would be excellent.'

I looked around.

This is a big church, I said.

'I know it,' he said, chuckling.

You have a New York accent.

'Um-hmm. Brooklyn.'

Was this your first assignment?

'Yes. When I first came, I was a deacon and a caretaker. I swept, mopped, vacuumed, cleaned the toilets.'

I thought of how the Reb, when he first arrived at our temple, had to help clean up and lock the doors. Maybe that's how Men of God develop humility.

'Long time ago,' Henry said, 'this was a famous

church. But a few years back, they sold it to our ministry. Actually, they said if you can pay the upkeep, it's yours.'

I glanced around.

Were you always going to be a pastor?

He snorted a laugh.

'Noooo.'

What did you plan on doing when you got out of school?

'Actually, I was in prison.'

Really? I said, acting casual. What for?

'Whoo, I did a lot of things. Drugs, stealing cars. I went to prison for manslaughter. Something I wasn't even involved in.'

And how did you get from that to this?

'Well . . . one night I thought I was going to be killed by some guys I stole from. So I made God a promise. If I lived to the morning. I would give myself to Him.'

He paused, as if some rusty old pain had just rumbled inside him. 'That was twenty years ago,' he said.

He patted his forehead with a handkerchief. 'I seen a lot in life. I know what the songwriter meant when he wrote, "Glory, Glory, hallelujah, since I laid my burden down."'

Okay, I said, because I didn't know what you say to that.

A few minutes later, we walked to the side exit. The floors were caked with grime. A stairway ran down to a small, dimly lit gymnasium, where, he told me, the homeless slept.

I was noncommittal about the charity help that day, saying I'd come back and we could talk more. To be honest, the prison thing was a red flag. I knew people could change. I also knew some people only changed locations.

Covering sports for a living – and living in Detroit – I had seen my share of bad behavior: drugs, assault, guns. I had witnessed 'apologies' in crowded press conferences. I interviewed men so adept at convincing you the trouble was behind them, that I would write laudatory stories – only to see the same men back in trouble a few months later.

In sports, it was bad enough. But I had a particular distaste for religious hypocrisy. Televangelists who solicited money, got arrested for lewd behavior, and soon were back soliciting under the guise of repentance – that stuff turned my stomach. I wanted to trust Henry Covington. But I didn't want to be naïve.

And then, let's be honest, his world of faith wasn't one I was used to. So broken down. So makeshift. The church seemed to sag even on the *inside*. The up staircase, Henry said, led to a floor where five tenants lived in dormlike rooms.

So, wait, people *live* in your church?

'Yes. A few. They pay a small rent.'

How do you pay your bills?

'Mostly from that.'

What about membership dues?
'There aren't any.'
Then how do you get paid a salary?
He laughed.
'I don't.'
We stepped out into the sun. The one-legged man was still there. He smiled. I forced a smile back.
Well, Pastor, I'll be in touch, I said.
I don't know if I meant it.
'You're welcome to come to service on Sunday,' he said.
I'm not Christian.
He shrugged. I couldn't tell if that meant okay, then you're not welcome, or okay, you still are.
Have you ever been in a synagogue? I asked.
'Yeah,' he said, 'when I was a teenager.'
What was the occasion?
He looked down sheepishly.
'We were robbing it.'

OCTOBER

OLD

The synagogue parking lot was jammed with cars, and the spillover stretched half a mile down the main road. It was Yom Kippur, the Day of Atonement, the holiest day of the Jewish calendar, the day when, it is said, the Lord decides who will be sealed in the Book of Life for another year.

Although solemn by any measure, this was always the Reb's shining hour, the morning for which his greatest sermons seemed reserved. It was rare when congregants did not go home buzzing about the Reb's message on life, death, love, forgiveness.

Not today. At eighty-nine, he had stopped giving sermons. He made no appearance on the pulpit. Instead, he sat quietly among the other worshippers, and I sat in the next section over, beside my father and mother, as I had done on this occasion all my life.

It was the one day I looked like I belonged.

At some point during the afternoon service, I walked over to find the Reb. I passed former

129

classmates, vaguely familiar faces but with thinning hair now, or eyeglasses, or jowls that didn't used to be there. They smiled and whispered hello, recalling me faster than I did them, and I wondered if deep down they thought I felt superior because I'd moved on. They might have been justified; I think I acted that way.

The Reb was sitting a few seats off the aisle, clapping along to an upbeat prayer. He wore a cream-colored robe, as usual, but his walker, which he hated to use in public, rested against the nearby wall. Sarah was next to him, and when she spotted me, she tapped her husband, who looked over from his clapping.

'Ahh,' he said. 'All the way from Detroit.'

His family members helped him up.

'Come. Let's talk.'

He eased out slowly, finding the walker. People in the aisle drew in, hands at the ready, in case he needed help. You could see in their faces the mix of reverence and concern.

He grabbed the handles and steered himself out.

Twenty minutes later, after stopping every few feet to greet somebody, we found seats in his small office, across from the large one he'd once inhabited. I had never before had a private audience with the Reb on the holiest day of the year. It felt strange being in his office when all those other people were outside.

'Your wife is here?' he asked.

With my folks, I said.

'Good.'

He had always been sweet to my wife. And he never chafed me over her faith. That was kind.

How are you feeling? I asked.

'Ach. They want me to eat today.'

Who?

'The doctors.'

It's okay.

'It isn't.' He clenched a fist. 'Today we fast. That is my tradition. I want to do what I always did.'

He lowered the fist, which shook on its own.

'You see?' he whispered. 'This is man's dilemma. We rail against it.'

Getting old?

'Getting old, we can deal with. *Being* old is the problem.'

One of the Reb's most memorable sermons, to me, anyhow, came after his oldest living relative, an aunt, had died. His mother and father were already gone, and his grandparents were long since buried. As he stood near his aunt's grave, he realized a simple but frightening thought:

I'm next.

What do you do when death's natural pecking order puts you in the front of the line, when you no longer can hide behind 'It's not my turn'?

Seeing the Reb now, slumped behind his desk, reminded me, sadly, of how long he had been on top of his family's list.

Why don't you do sermons anymore? I asked.

'I can't bear the thought,' he said, sighing. 'If I stumbled on a word. If, at a key moment, I should lose my place—'

You don't need to be embarrassed.

'Not me,' he corrected. 'The people. If they see me discombobulated . . . it reminds them that I'm dying. I don't want to scare them like that.'

I should have known he was thinking of us.

As a child, I truly believed there was a Book of Life, some huge, dusty thing in a library in the sky, and once a year, on the Day of Atonement, God flipped through the pages with a feathered quill pen and – *check, check, X, check* – you lived or you died. I was always afraid that I wasn't praying hard enough, that I needed to shut my eyes tighter to will God's pen from one side to the other.

What do people fear most about death? I asked the Reb.

'Fear?' He thought for a moment. 'Well, for one thing, what happens next? Where do we go? Is it what we imagined?'

That's big.

'Yes. But there's something else.'

What else?

He leaned forward.

'Being forgotten,' he whispered.

There is a cemetery not far from my house, with graves that date back to the nineteenth century.

I have never seen anyone come there to lay a flower. Most people just wander through, read the engravings, and say, 'Wow. Look how *old*.'

That cemetery came to mind in the Reb's office, after he quoted a poem both beautiful and heart-breaking. Written by Thomas Hardy, it told of a man among tombstones, conversing with the dead below. The recently buried souls lamented the older souls that had already slid from memory:

> *They count as quite forgot,*
> *They are as men who have existed not,*
> *Theirs is a loss past loss of fitful breath*
> *It is the second death.*

The second death. The unvisited in nursing homes. The homeless found frozen in alleys. Who mourned their passing? Who marked their time on earth?

'Once, on a trip to Russia,' the Reb recalled, 'we found an old Orthodox synagogue. Inside, there was an elderly man, standing alone, saying the mourner's Kaddish. Being polite, we asked for whom he was saying it. He looked up and answered, "I am saying it for myself."'

The second death. To think that you died and no one would remember you. I wondered if this was why we tried so hard to make our mark in America. To be *known*. Think of how important celebrity has become. We sing to get famous; expose our worst secrets to get famous; lose

133

weight, eat bugs, even commit murder to get famous. Our young people post their deepest thoughts on public Web sites. They run cameras from their bedrooms. It's as if we are screaming, *Notice me! Remember me!* Yet the notoriety barely lasts. Names quickly blur and in time are forgotten.

How then, I asked the Reb, can you avoid the second death?

'In the short run,' he said, 'the answer is simple. Family. It is through my family that I hope to live on for a few generations. When they remember me, I live on. When they pray for me, I live on. All the memories we have made, the laughs and the tears.

'But that, too, is limited.'

How so?

He sang the next sentence.

'Ifff . . . I've done a good jobbb, then I'll be re-mem-bered one generation, maybe two . . . but e-ven-tu-allllly . . . they're gonna say, "What was his naaame again?"'

At first I protested. Then I stopped. I realized I did not know my great-grandmother's name. I'd never seen my great-grandfather's face. How many generations does it take, even in close-knit families, for the fabric to unravel?

'This is why,' the Reb said, 'faith is so important. It is a rope for us all to grab, up and down the mountain. I may not be remembered in so many years.

134

But what I believe and have taught – about God, about our tradition – *that* can go on. It comes from my parents and their parents before them. And if it stretches to my grandchildren and to their grand- children, then we are all, you know . . .'

Connected?

'That's it.'

We should get back to services, I said.

'All right. Yes. Gimme a little shove here.'

I realized it was just me there, and he couldn't get up from the chair without help. How far was this from the days when he commanded the pulpit with a booming voice and I sat in the crowd, wowed by his performance? I tried not to think about that. I awkwardly moved behind him, counted 'one . . . two . . . three,' then lifted him by the elbows.

'Ahhhh,' he exhaled. 'Old, old, old.'

I bet you could still do a helluva sermon.

He grabbed the walker's handles. He paused.

'You think so?' he asked, softly.

Yeah, I said. No question.

*I*n the basement of his house there are old film reels of the Reb, Sarah, and their family:

Here they are in the early 1950s, bouncing their first child, Shalom.

Here they are a few years later with their twin girls, Orah and Rinah.

Here they are in 1960, pushing Gilah, their youngest, in her baby carriage.

Although the footage is grainy, the expressions of delight on the Reb's face – holding, hugging, and kissing his children – are unmistakable. He seems predestined to raise a family. He never hits his kids. He rarely raises his voice. He makes memories in small, loving bites: slow afternoon walks home from temple, nights doing homework with his daughters, long Sabbath dinners of family conversation, summer days throwing a baseball backward over his head to his son.

Once, he drives Shalom and a few of his young friends over the bridge from Philadelphia. As they approach the toll booth, he asks if the boys have their passports.

'Passports?' they say.

'You mean you don't have your passports – and you expect to get into New Jersey?' he cries. 'Quick! Hide under that blanket! Don't breathe! Don't make a sound!'

Later, he teases them about the whole thing. But under that blanket, in the back of a car, another family story is forged, one that father and son will laugh about for decades. This is how a legacy is built. One memory at a time.

His kids are grown now. His son is an established rabbi. His oldest daughter is a library director; his youngest, a teacher. They each have children of their own.

'We have this photograph, all of us together,' the Reb says. 'Whenever I feel the spirit of death hovering, I look at that picture, the whole family smiling at the camera. And I say, "Al, you done okay.

'"This is your immortality."'

CHURCH

As I entered the church, a thin man with a high forehead nodded and gave me a small white envelope in case I wished to make a donation. He motioned for me to take a seat anywhere. The weather had turned to a blowing rain, and the hole in the ceiling loomed overhead, dark and dripping, the red buckets on plywood planks to catch the incoming water.

The pews were mostly empty. Up front, near the altar, a man sat behind a portable organ and occasionally hit a chord, which was punctuated with a rim shot – *pwock!* – by a drummer. Their small music echoed in the big room.

Standing to the side was Pastor Henry, in a long blue robe, swaying back and forth. After several of his entreaties, I had come to a service. I'm not sure why. Maybe curiosity. Maybe, to be blunt, to see if I trusted him for the charity contribution. We had spoken several times now. He had spared no detail of his criminal history – the drugs, the guns, the jail time – and while it was nice that he was honest, if you went strictly on his past, there might be no reason to invest in his future.

But there was also something sad and confessional in his face, something weary in his voice, as if he'd had enough of the world, or at least certain parts of it. And while I couldn't help but think of that old expression 'Never trust a fat preacher,' I had little concern that Henry Covington was siphoning profits from his congregation. There were none to be had.

He looked up from his meditation and saw me. Then he continued praying.

Henry Covington was sent to Detroit in 1992 by Bishop Roy Brown of the Pilgrim Assemblies International in New York. Brown had discovered Henry in his church, had heard his testimony, and had taken him to prisons and watched the way inmates reacted to his story. Eventually, after training him, teaching him, and ordaining him a deacon, he asked Henry to go to the Motor City.

Henry would have done anything for Brown. He moved his family into a Ramada Inn in downtown Detroit and was paid three hundred dollars a week to help build a new Pilgrim ministry. His transportation was an old black limousine that Bishop Brown granted him, in part to ferry the man around when he came to town for weekend services.

Over the years, Henry served under three different pastors, and each one noted his devotion to study and his easy connection to people in the neighborhood. They elevated him to elder and finally pastor. But eventually the Pilgrim interest faded, Bishop Brown stopped coming, and so did Henry's money.

He had to sink or swim on his own.

His house went into foreclosure. The sheriffs put a sign on the door. His water and electricity were turned off. Meanwhile, the ignored church had a busted boiler and cracked pipes. There were local drug dealers who let it be known that if Henry let the place serve as a secret distribution center, his financial woes could go away.

But Henry was done with that life.

So he dug in. He formed the I Am My Brother's Keeper Ministry, he asked God for guidance, and he did whatever he could to keep his church and his family afloat.

Now, as the organ played, someone hobbled forward on crutches. It was the one-legged man from my first visit. His nickname was Cass, short for Anthony Castelow. It turned out he was a church elder.

'Thank you, thank you, Lord,' he began, his eyes nearly closed, 'thank you, thank you, thank you . . .'

Someone clapped. Someone yelled, 'Well . . .' which came out more like 'Way-elll.' You could hear the traffic noise through the doors when they opened.

'Thank you, Jesus . . . thank you for our pastor, thank you for the day . . .'

I counted twenty-six people, all African-American, mostly female. I sat behind an older woman who wore a dress the color of a Caribbean sea, with a wide hat to match. As crowds went, it was a far cry from those megachurches in California, or even a suburban synagogue.

'Thank you for this day, thank you, Jesus . . .'

When Elder Cass finished, he turned to go, but the cord got caught in his crutch and the microphone hit the floor with an amplified *phwock*.

A woman quickly put it right.

Then the sanctuary quieted.

And with his cheeks and forehead already shiny with perspiration, Pastor Henry came forward.

The moment a cleric rises for a sermon is, for me, a time for the body to ease in, as if the good listening is about to start. I had always done this with the Reb, and, out of habit, I slid down in the wooden pew as the organist held the last chords of 'Amazing Grace.'

Henry leaned forward toward the people. He held there, for a moment, as if pondering one last thought. Then he spoke.

'Amazing grace . . . ,' he said, shaking his head. '. . . Amaaaa-zing grace.'

Someone repeated, 'Amazing grace!' Others clapped. Clearly, this wasn't going to be the quiet, reflective audience I was used to.

'Amaaaazing grace,' Henry bellowed. 'I coulda been dead.'

'*Mmm-hmm!*'

'Shoulda been dead!'

'*Mmm-hmm!*'

'Woulda been dead! . . . But his grace!'

'*Yes!*'

'*His* grace . . . saved a wretch. And I was a wretch. You know what a wretch is? I was a crackhead, an alcoholic, I was a heroin addict, a liar, a thief. I was *all* those things. But then came Jesus—'

'*Jesus!*'

'I call him the greatest recycler I know! . . . Jesus . . . he lifts me up. He rearranges me. He *repositions* me. By myself, I'm no good—'

'*Way-ell—*'

'But he makes all the difference!'

'*Amen to that!*'

'Now, yesterday . . . yesterday, friends, a portion of the ceiling done fell down. It was leaking in the sanctuary. But you know—'

'*Tell it, Rev—*'

'You know-you-know-you-know . . . how that song go . . . Hallelujah—'

'*Hallelujah!*'

'Anyhow!'

He began to clap. The organist joined in. The drummer right behind him. And off they went, as if a floodlight had just ignited the altar.

'*Haaaa-llelujah anyhow . . .*' Henry sang, '*. . . never gonna let life's troubles get you down . . .*

'*No matter what comes your way,*

'Lift your voice and say—
'Hallelujah . . . anyhow!'

His voice was beautiful, pure and crisp and almost too high-pitched, it seemed, to come from such a large man. The whole congregation was immediately engaged, inspired, clapping, dipping shoulders and singing along – all except me. I felt like the loser who got left out of the choir.

'Hal-le-lujah . . . anyhow!'

When the song stopped, Henry picked right back up with his preaching. There was no line between prayer, hymn, word, song, preach, beseech, or call and respond. It was apparently all part of the package.

'We were in here last night,' Henry said, 'just looking around, looking around, and the plaster was peeling and the paint was chipping everywhere—'

'Sure is!'

'And you could hear the water pouring in. We had buckets all over. And I asked the Lord. I began to pray. I said, "Lord, show us your mercy and your kindness. Help us heal your house. Just help us fix this hole—"'

'All right now—'

'And for a few minutes, I despaired. Because I don't know where the money will come from to fix it. But then I stopped.'

'That's right!'

'I stopped, because I realized something.'

'Yes, Rev!'

'The Lord, you see, he's interested in what you do, but the Lord don't care nothing about no building.'

'*Amen!*'

'The Lord don't care nothing about no *building!*'

'*That's RIGHT!*'

'Jesus said, "Therefore do not worry about tomorrow, for tomorrow will worry about itself." God don't care about no *building*. He cares about you, and what's in your heart.'

'*Lord of Hosts!*'

'And if this is the place where we come to worship – if this is the place where we come to worship . . . if this is the *only place we can come to worship . . .*'

He paused. His voice lowered to a whisper.

'Then it is holy to *him.*'

'*Yes, Rev! . . . Preach it, Pastor! . . . Amen! . . . Way-ell!*'

The people rose and clapped enthusiastically, convinced, thanks to Henry, that while their building might be disintegrating, their souls were still in sight, and perhaps the Lord was using that roof hole to peer down and help them.

I looked up and saw the red buckets and the water dripping. I saw Henry stepping back, in his huge blue robe, singing along in prayer. I wasn't sure what to make of him – charismatic, enigmatic, problematic? But you had to figure his mother was right all along. He was going to be a preacher, no matter how long it took.

I *begin to read about faiths beyond my own. I am
curious to see if they aren't more similar than I
had believed. I read about Mormons, Catholics,
Sufis, Quakers.*

*I come upon a documentary about the Hindu cele-
bration of Kumbh Mela, a holy pilgrimage from the
mouth of the Ganges River to its source in the
Himalayas. The legend is that four drops of immortal
nectar were dropped when the gods fought with the
demons in the sky, and that nectar landed in four
places on earth. The pilgrimage is a journey to those
places; to bathe in the river waters, to wash away
sins, and to seek health and salvation.*

*Millions attend. Tens of millions. It is an incredible
sight. I see bearded men dancing. I see holy men with
pierced lips and powdered skin. I see elderly women
who have traveled for weeks to seek the majesty of
God in the snowcapped mountains.*

*It is the largest gathering of humanity on earth
and has been called 'the world's largest single act
of faith.' Yet for most in my country, it is totally
alien. The documentary refers to Kumbh Mela as*

'being part of something big while doing something small.'

I wonder if that applies to visiting an old man in New Jersey?

A GOOD MARRIAGE

I haven't said a lot about the Reb's wife. I should.

According to Jewish tradition, forty days before a male baby is born, a heavenly voice shouts out whom he will marry. If so, the name 'Sarah' was yelled for Albert sometime in 1917. Their union was long, loving, and resilient.

They met through a job interview in Brighton Beach – he was a principal, she was seeking an English teacher's job – and they disagreed on several issues and she left thinking, *'There goes* that *job;'* but he hired her and admired her. And eventually, months later, he asked her into his office.

'Are you seeing anyone romantically?' he inquired.

'No, I'm not,' she replied.

'Good. Please keep it that way. Because I intend to ask you to marry me.'

She hid her amusement.

'Anything else?' she said.

'No,' he answered.

'Okay.' And she left.

★ ★ ★

It took months for him to follow up, his shyness having taken over, but he did, eventually, and they courted. He took her to a restaurant. He took her to Coney Island. The first time he tried to kiss her, he got hiccups.

Two years later, they were married.

In more than six decades together, Albert and Sarah Lewis raised four children, buried one, danced at their kids' weddings, attended their parents' funerals, welcomed seven grandchildren, lived in just three houses, and never stopped supporting, debating, loving, and cherishing each other. They might argue, even give each other the silent treatment, but their children would see them at night, through the door, sitting on the edge of the bed, holding hands.

They truly were a team. From the pulpit, the Reb might zing her with, 'Excuse me, young lady, could you tell us your name?' She would get him back by telling people, 'I've had thirty wonderful years with my husband, and I'll never forget the day we were married, November 3, 1944.'

'Wait . . .,' someone would say, doing the math, 'that's way more than thirty years ago.'

'Right,' she would say. 'On Monday you get twenty great minutes, on Tuesday you get a great hour. You put it all together, you get thirty great years.'

Everyone would laugh, and her husband would beam. In a list of suggestions for young clerics, the Reb had once written 'find a good partner.'

He had found his.

And just as harvests make you wise to farming, so did years of matrimony enlighten the Reb as to how a marriage works – and doesn't. He had officiated at nearly a thousand weddings, from the most basic to the embarrassingly garish. Many couples lasted. Many did not.

Can you predict which marriages will survive? I asked.

'Sometimes,' he said. 'If they're communicating well, they have a good chance. If they have a similar belief system, similar values, they have a good chance.'

What about love?

'Love they should always have. But love changes.'

What do you mean?

'Love – the infatuation kind – "he's so handsome, she's so beautiful" – that can shrivel. As soon as something goes wrong, that kind of love can fly out the window.

'On the other hand, a true love can enrich itself. It gets tested and grows stronger. Like in *Fiddler on the Roof.* You remember? When Tevye sings "Do You Love Me?"?'

I should have seen this coming. I think *Fiddler on the Roof* was pretty much the Reb's worldview. Religion. Tradition. Community. And a husband

and wife – Tevye and Golde – whose love is proven through action, not words.

'When she says, "How can you ask if I love you? Look at all I've done with you. What else would you call it?"

'*That* kind of love – the kind you realize you already have by the life you've created together – that's the kind that lasts.'

The Reb was lucky to have such a love with Sarah. It had endured hardships by relying on cooperation – and selflessness. The Reb was fond of telling young couples, 'Remember, the only difference between "marital" and "martial" is where you put the "i."'

He also, on occasion, told the joke about a man who complains to his doctor that his wife, when angry, gets historical.

'You mean hysterical,' the doctor says.

'No, historical,' the man says. 'She lists the *history* of every wrong thing I've ever done!'

Still, the Reb knew that marriage was an endangered institution. He'd officiated for couples, seen them split, then officiated when they married someone else.

'I think people expect too much from marriage today,' he said. 'They expect perfection. Every moment should be bliss. That's TV or movies. But that is not the human experience.

'Like Sarah says, twenty good minutes here, forty good minutes there, it adds up to something beautiful. The trick is when things aren't so great, you don't junk the whole thing. It's okay to have an argument. It's okay that the other one nudges you a little, bothers you a little. It's part of being close to someone.

'But the joy you get from that same closeness – when you watch your children, when you wake up and smile at each other – that, as our tradition teaches us, is a blessing. People forget that.'

Why do they forget it?

'Because the word "commitment" has lost its meaning. I'm old enough to remember when it used to be a positive. A committed person was someone to be admired. He was loyal and steady. Now a commitment is something you avoid. You don't want to tie yourself down.

'It's the same with faith, by the way. We don't want to get stuck having to go to services all the time, or having to follow all the rules. We don't want to commit to God. We'll take Him when we need Him, or when things are going good. But real commitment? That requires staying power – in faith and in marriage.'

And if you don't commit? I asked.

'Your choice. But you miss what's on the other side.'

What's on the other side?

'Ah.' He smiled. 'A happiness you cannot find alone.'

★　★　★

151

Moments later, Sarah entered the room, wearing her coat. Like her husband, she was in her eighties, had thick, whitening hair, wore glasses, and had a disarming smile.

'I'm going shopping, Al,' she said.

'All right. We will miss you.' He crossed his hands over his stomach, and for a moment they just grinned at each other.

I thought about their commitment, sixty-plus years. I thought about how much he relied on her now. I pictured them at night, holding hands on the edge of the bed. *A happiness you cannot find alone.*

'I was going to ask you a question,' the Reb told his wife.

'Which is?'

'Well . . . I've already forgotten.'

'Okay,' she laughed. 'The answer is no.'

'Or *maybe* no?'

'Or maybe no.'

She walked over and playfully shook his hand.

'So, it was nice to meet you.'

He laughed. 'It was a pleasure.'

They kissed.

I don't know about forty days before you're born, but at that moment, it wouldn't have surprised me to hear two names shouted from the heavens.

*A*s a child, I am certain I will never marry out of my religion.

As an adult, I do it anyhow.

My wife and I are wed on a Caribbean island. The sun is going down, the weather is warm and lovely. Her family reads Bible passages. My siblings sing a funny tribute. I step on a glass. We are married by a local female magistrate, who offers us her own private blessing.

Although we come from different faiths, we forge a loving solution: I support her, she supports me, we attend each other's religious functions, and while we both stand silent during certain prayers, we always say 'Amen.'

Still, there are moments: when she is troubled, she asks Jesus for help, and I hear her pray quietly and I feel locked out. When you intermarry, you mix more than two people – you mix histories, traditions, you mix the Holy Communion stories and the Bar Mitzvah photos. And even though, as she sometimes says, 'I believe in the Old Testament; we're not that different,' we are different.

Are you angry with me about my marriage? I ask the Reb.

'Why would I be angry?' he says. 'What would anger do? Your wife is a wonderful person. You love each other. I see that.'

Then how do you square that with your job?

'Well. If one day you came and said, "Guess what? She wants to convert to Judaism," I wouldn't be upset. Until then . . .'

He sang. 'Until then, we'll all get alonnng . . .'

LIFE OF HENRY

I couldn't help but compare the Reb and Pastor Henry now and then. Both loved to sing. Both delivered a mean sermon. Like the Reb, Henry had been shepherd to just one congregation his whole career and husband to just one wife. And like Albert and Sarah Lewis, Henry and Annette Covington had a son and two daughters, and had also lost a child.

But after that, their stories veered apart.

Henry, for example, didn't meet his future wife at a job interview. He first saw Annette when she was shooting dice.

'Come on, six!' she yelled, throwing the bones against a stoop with his older brother. 'Six dice! Gimme a six!'

She was fifteen, Henry was sixteen, and he was smitten, totally gone, like those cartoons where Cupid shoots an arrow with a *boinngg!* You might not view a dice roll as romantic, and it may not seem a fitting way for a Man of God to find a lasting love, but at nineteen, when Henry went to prison, he told Annette, 'I don't expect you to wait seven years,' and she said, 'If it was twenty-five years, I'd still be here.' So who is to say what a lasting love looks like?

Every weekend during Henry's incarceration, Annette rode a bus that left the city around midnight and took six hours to reach upstate New York. She was there when the sun came up, and when visiting hours began, she and Henry held hands and played cards and talked until those hours were over. She rarely missed a weekend, despite the grueling schedule, and she kept his spirits up by giving him something to look forward to. Henry's mother sent him a letter while he was locked up, saying if he did not stay with Annette, 'you might find another woman, but you will never find your wife.'

They were married when he got out, in a simple ceremony at Mt. Moriah Church. He was slim then, handsome and tall; she wore her hair in bangs, and her high smile gleamed in the wedding photos. There was a reception at a nightclub called Sagittarius. They spent the weekend at a hotel in the garment district. Monday morning. Annette was back at work.

She was twenty-two. Henry was twenty-three. Within a year, they would lose a baby, lose a job, and see the boiler in their apartment burst in winter, leaving them with icicles hanging from their ceiling.

And then the real trouble started.

The Reb said that a good marriage should endure tribulations, and Henry and Annette's had done that. But early on, those 'tribulations' were drug abuse, crime, and avoiding the police. Not exactly *Fiddler on the Roof*. Both Henry and Annette had been addicts, who cleaned up once Henry came home from prison. But after their baby died and the boiler burst and Annette lost her job – and a broke Henry saw his drug-dealing brother with a fat bankroll of hundred-dollar bills – they fell back into that life, and they fell all the way. Henry sold drugs at parties. He sold them from his house. Soon the customers were so frequent, he made them wait on the corner and come up one at a time. He and Annette became heavy users and drinkers, and they lived in fear of both the police and rival drug lords. One night, Henry was taken for a ride with some Manhattan dealers, a ride he thought might end in his death; Annette was waiting with gun in hand if he didn't come back.

But when Henry finally hit bottom – that night behind those trash cans – Annette did, too.

'What's keeping you from going to God?' Henry asked her that Easter morning.

'You are,' she admitted.

The next week, he and Annette got rid of the drugs and the guns. They threw away the paraphernalia. They went back to church and read the Bible nightly. They fought back periodic weaknesses and helped one another get through.

One morning, a few months into this rehabilitation, there was a knock at their door. It was very early. A man's voice said he wanted to buy some product.

Henry, in bed, shouted for him to go away, he didn't do that anymore. The man persisted. Henry yelled, 'There ain't nothing in here!' The man kept knocking. Henry got out of bed, pulled a sheet around himself, and went to the door.

'I told you—'

'Don't move!' a voice barked.

Henry was staring at five police officers, their guns drawn.

'Step away,' one said.

They pushed through his door. They told Annette to freeze. They searched the entire place, top to bottom, warning the couple that if they had anything incriminating, they had better tell them now. Henry knew everything was gone, but his heart was racing. *Did I miss anything?* He glanced around. *Nothing there. Nothing there—*

Oh, no.

Suddenly, he couldn't swallow. It felt like a baseball was in his throat. Sitting on an end table, one atop the other, were two red notebooks. One, Henry knew, contained Bible verses from Proverbs, which he had been writing down every night. The other was older. It contained names, transactions, and dollar amounts of hundreds of drug deals.

He had taken out the old notebook to destroy it. Now it could destroy him. An officer wandered over. He lifted one of the notebooks and opened it. Henry's knees went weak. His lungs pounded. The man's eyes moved up and down the page. Then he threw it down and moved on.

Proverbs, apparently, didn't interest him.

An hour later, when the police left, Henry and Annette grabbed the old notebook, burned it immediately, and spent the rest of the day thanking God.

What would you do if your clergyman told you stories like that? There was part of me that admired Henry's honesty, and part that felt his laundry list of bad behavior should somehow disqualify him from the pulpit. Still, I had heard him preach several times now, citing the Book of Acts, the Beatitudes, Solomon, Queen Esther, and Jesus telling his disciples that 'anyone who loses his life for me shall find it again.' Henry's gospel singing was inspired and engaged. And he always seemed to be around the church, either up in his second-floor office – a long, narrow room with a conference table left over from the previous tenants – or in the small, dimly lit gymnasium. One afternoon I walked into the sanctuary, unannounced, and he was sitting there, hands crossed, his eyes closed in prayer.

Before the weather turned cold, Henry occasionally cooked on a grill by the side of the church; chicken, shrimp, whatever he could get donated. He gave it out to whoever was hungry. He even preached sometimes on a low crumbling concrete wall across the street.

'I've spread as much of God's word on that wall,' Henry said one day, 'as I have inside.'

How is that?

159

'Because some people aren't ready to come in. Maybe they feel guilty, on accounta what they're up to. So I go out there, bring them a sandwich.'

Kind of like a house call?

'Yeah. Except most of 'em don't have houses.'

Are some of them on drugs?

'Oh, yeah. But so are some folks coming in on Sundays.'

You're kidding. During your service?

'Whoo, yeah. I'm looking right at them. You see that head whoppin' and boppin' and you say, "Umm-hmm, they had something powerful."'

That doesn't bother you?

'Not at all. You know what I tell them? I don't care if you're drunk, or you just left the drug house, I don't care. When I'm sick, I go to the emergency room. And if the problem continues, I go again. So whatever's ailing you, let this church be your emergency room. Until you get the healing, don't stop coming.'

I studied Henry's wide, soft face.

Can I ask you something? I said.

'Okay.'

What did you rob from that synagogue?

He exhaled and laughed. 'Believe it or not – envelopes.'

Envelopes?

'That's it. I was just a teenager. Some older guys had broken in before me and stolen anything valuable. All I found was a box of envelopes. I took 'em and ran out.'

Do you even remember what you did with them? 'No,' he answered. 'I sure don't.'

I looked at him, looked at his church, and wondered if one man's life ever truly makes sense to another.

I take home a box of the Reb's old sermons. I leaf
through them. There is one from the 1950s on
'The Purpose of a Synagogue' and one from the
1960s called 'The Generation Gap.'

I see one entitled 'Raindrops Keep Falling on My
Head.' It is from the late 1970s. I read it. I do a double
take.

It is an appeal to fix the collapsing roof.

'Our roof sheds copious tears after each rain,' the Reb
wrote. He mentioned sitting in the sanctuary when a
'sodden wet ceiling tile' fell and just missed him, and a
wedding celebration in which two days of rain 'created
unwanted gravy on the chicken.' During a morning
service, he had to grab a broom and puncture a buck-
ling tile to allow the rainwater to gush through.

In the sermon, he beseeches members to give more
to keep their house of worship from literally caving in.

I think about Pastor Henry and his roof hole. It is
the first time I see a connection. An inner-city church.
A suburban synagogue.

Then again, our congregation ultimately came up
with the money. And Henry couldn't even ask his.

NOVEMBER

YOUR FAITH, MY FAITH

When I was a teenager, the Reb did a sermon that made me laugh. He read a thank-you letter from another clergyman. At the end, it was signed: 'May your god – and our god – bless you.'

I laughed at the idea that two Almightys could be sent the same message. I was too young to realize the more serious shadings of that distinction.

Once I moved to the Midwest – to an area some nicknamed the 'Northern Bible Belt' – the issue became weightier. I had strangers tell me 'God bless you' in the grocery store. What should I say to that? I interviewed athletes who credited their 'Lord and savior, Jesus Christ' for touchdowns or home runs. I worked volunteer projects with Hindus, Buddhists, Catholics. And because metro Detroit boasts the largest Arab population outside of the Middle East, Muslim issues were a regular part of life, including a debate over a local mosque broadcasting *Adhan*, the daily call to prayer, in a largely Polish neighborhood that already rang with church bells.

In other words, 'May your god and our god bless you' – and whose god was blessing whom – had gone from funny to controversial to confrontational. I found myself keeping quiet. Almost hiding. I think many people in minority religions do this. Part of the reason I drifted from my faith was that I didn't want to feel defensive about it. A pathetic reason, looking back, but true.

One Sunday, not long before Thanksgiving, I took the train from New York, entered the Reb's house, greeted him with a hug, and trooped behind him to his office, his metal walker leading the way. It now had a small basket in front, which contained a few books and, for some reason, a red maraca gourd.

'I have found that if the walker looks like a shopping cart,' the Reb said, mischievously, 'the congregation is more comfortable.'

His eulogy request now sat like a term paper in my mind. On some visits, I felt I had forever to finish it; on others, I felt I had days, not even weeks. Today, the Reb seemed well, his eyes clear, his voice strong, which reassured me. Once we sat, I told him about the homeless charity and even the rescue mission where I'd spent the night.

I wasn't sure I should mention a Christian mission to a rabbi, and the moment I said it, I felt guilty, like a traitor. I remembered a story the Reb had told me once about taking his old-world grandmother to a baseball game. When everyone jumped and cheered at a home run, she stayed seated. He turned and asked why she wasn't clapping for the big hit. And she said to him, in Yiddish, 'Albert, is it good for the Jews?'

My worry was wasted. The Reb made no such value judgments. 'Our faith tells us to do charitable acts and to aid the poor in our community,' he said. 'That is being righteous, no matter who you help.'

Soon we had tumbled into a most fundamental debate. How can different religions coexist? If one faith believes one thing, and another believes something else, how can they both be correct? And does one religion have the right – or even the obligation – to try to convert the other?

The Reb had been living with these issues all of his professional life. 'In the early 1950s,' he recalled, 'our congregation's kids used to wrap their Jewish books in brown paper before they got on the bus. Remember, to many around here, we were the first Jewish people they had ever seen.'

Did that make for some strange moments?

He chuckled. 'Oh, yes. I remember one time a congregant came to me all upset, because her son, the only Jewish boy in his class, had been cast in the school's Christmas play. And they cast him as Jesus.

'So I went to the teacher. I explained the dilemma. And she said, "But that's *why* we chose him, Rabbi. Because Jesus was a *Jew!*"'

I remembered similar incidents. In elementary

school, I was left out of the big, colorful Christmas productions of 'God Rest Ye Merry Gentlemen' or 'Jingle Bells.' Instead, I had to join the school's few other Jewish kids onstage, as we sang the Hanukah song, 'Dreidel, Dreidel, Dreidel, I Made It Out of Clay.' We held hands and moved in a circle, imitating a spinning top. No props. No costumes. At the end of the song, we all fell down.

I swear I saw some gentile parents hiding their laughter.

Is there any winning a religious argument? Whose God is better than whose? Who got the Bible right or wrong? I preferred figures like Rajchandra, the Indian poet who influenced Gandhi by teaching that no religion was superior because they all brought people closer to God; or Gandhi himself, who would break a fast with Hindu prayers, Muslim quotations, or a Christian hymn.

Over the years, the Reb had lived his beliefs, but never tried to convert anyone to them. As a general rule, Judaism does not seek converts. In fact, the tradition is to first discourage them, emphasizing the difficulties and suffering the religion has endured.

This is not the case with all religions. Throughout history, countless millions have been slaughtered for failing to convert, to accept another god, or to denounce their own beliefs. Rabbi Akiva, the famous second-century scholar, was tortured to death by the Romans for refusing to give up his religious study. As they raked his flesh with iron combs, he whispered his final words on earth, 'Hear, oh Israel, the Lord our God, the Lord is One.' He died with the word 'one' on his lips.

That prayer – and the word 'one' – were integral to the Reb's beliefs. One, as in the singular God. One, as in the Lord's creation, Adam.

'Ask yourself, "Why did God create but one man?"' the Reb said, wagging a finger. 'Why, if he meant for there to be faiths bickering with each other, didn't he create that from the start? He created trees, right? Not one tree, countless trees. Why not the same with man?

'Because we are all from that one man – and all from that one God. That's the message.'

Then why, I asked, is the world so fractured?

'Well, you can look at it this way. Would you want the world to all look alike? No. The genius of life is its variety.

'Even in our own faith, we have questions and answers, interpretations, debates. In Christianity, in Catholicism, in other faiths, the same thing – debates, interpretations. That is the beauty. It's like being a musician. If you found *the* note, and you kept hitting that note all the time, you would go nuts. It's the blending of the different notes that makes the music.'

The music of what?

'Of believing in something bigger than yourself.'

But what if someone from another faith won't recognize yours? Or wants you dead for it?

'That is not faith. That is hate.' He sighed. 'And if you ask me, God sits up there and cries when that happens.'

He coughed, then, as if to reassure me, he smiled. He had fulltime help at the house now; his home care workers had included a tall woman from Ghana and a burly Russian man. Now, on weekdays, there was a lovely Hindu woman from Trinidad named Teela. She helped get him dressed and do some light exercises in the morning, fixed his meals, and drove him to the supermarket and synagogue. Sometimes she would play Hindi religious music over her car stereo. The Reb enjoyed it and asked for a translation. When she talked about reincarnation, per her faith, he quizzed her and apologized for not knowing more about Hinduism over the years.

How can you – a cleric – be so open-minded? I asked.

'Look. I know what I believe. It's in my soul. But I constantly tell our people: you should be convinced of the *authenticity* of what you have, but you must also be humble enough to say that we don't know everything. And since we don't know everything, we must accept that another person may believe something else.'

He sighed.

'I'm not being original here, Mitch. Most religions teach us to love our neighbor.'

I thought about how much I admired him at

168

that moment. How he never, even in private, even in old age, tried to bully another belief, or bad-mouth someone else's devotion. And I realized I had been a bit of a coward on this whole faith thing. I should have been more proud, less intimidated. I shouldn't have bitten my tongue. If the only thing wrong with Moses is that he's not yours; if the only thing wrong with Jesus is that he's not yours; if the only thing wrong with mosques, Lent, chanting, Mecca, Buddha, confession, or reincarnation is that they're not yours – well, maybe the problem is you.

One more question? I asked the Reb.

He nodded.

When someone from another faith says, 'God bless you,' what do you say?

'I say, "Thank you, and God bless you, too."'

Really?

'Why shouldn't I?'

I went to answer and realized I had no answer. No answer at all.

I read up on Buddhist stories and parables.

One concerns a farmer who wakes up to find that his horse has run off.

The neighbors come by and say, 'Too bad. Such awful luck.'

The farmer says, 'Maybe.'

The next day, the horse returns with a few other horses. The neighbors congratulate the farmer on his reversal of fortune.

'Maybe,' the farmer says.

When his son tries to ride one of the new horses, he breaks his leg, and the neighbors offer condolences.

'Maybe,' the farmer says.

And the next day, when army officials come to draft the son – and don't take him because of his broken leg – everyone is happy.

'Maybe,' the farmer says.

I have heard stories like this before. They are beautiful in their simplicity and surrender to the universe. I wonder if I could be attached to something so detached. I don't know. Maybe.

THE THINGS WE FIND . . .

After leaving the Reb's house, I stopped at the synagogue, seeking information on the original building back in the 1940s.

'That might be in our files,' a woman had told me over the phone.

I didn't know there were files, I'd said.

'We have files on everything. We have a file on you.'

You're kidding. Can I see it?

'You can have it if you want.'

Now I walked into the foyer. The religious school was still in session, and there were kids everywhere. The preteen girls loped with awkward self-awareness, and the boys ran the halls and grabbed their heads to keep their yarmulkes from falling off.

Nothing had changed, I thought. Usually, this would make me feel superior. I had soared away while the poor hometown kids were doing the same old thing. But this time, I don't know why, all I felt was empty distance.

Hi, I said to a woman behind the desk. My name is—

'Come on, we know you. Here's the file.'

I blinked. I almost forgot that my family had been part of this place for four decades.

Thanks, I said.

'Sure thing.'

I took the file on me and headed home, or to the place I called home now.

On the plane I leaned back and undid a rubber band that held the file's contents. I reflected on my life since New Jersey. My plans as a young man – my 'citizen of the world' dreams – had come true, to a degree. I had friends in different time zones. I'd had books published in foreign languages. I'd had many addresses over the years.

But you can touch everything and be connected to nothing. I knew airports better than I knew local neighborhoods. I knew more names in other area codes than I did on my block. The 'community' I had joined was the community of the workplace. Friends were through work. Conversation was about work. Most of my socialization came through work.

And in recent months, those workplace pillars had been falling down. Friends were laid off. Downsized. They took buyouts. Offices closed. People who were always in one place were no longer there when you called. They sent e-mails saying they were exploring 'exciting new options.' I never believed the 'exciting' part.

And without the work connection, the human ties

released, like magnets losing their attraction. We promised to keep up, but the promises were not kept. Some people behaved as if unemployment were contagious. Anyhow, without the commonality of work – the complaints, the gossip – how much was there to talk about?

When I dumped the contents of my personal file onto the tray table, I found report cards, old papers, even a religious school play I wrote in fourth grade on Queen Esther:

MORDECHI: ESTHER!
ESTHER: YES, UNCLE?
MORDECHI: GO TO THE CASTLE.
ESTHER: BUT I HAVE NOTHING TO WEAR!

There were also copies of congratulatory letters from the Reb – some handwritten – on getting into college, on my engagement. I felt ashamed. He had tried to stay in touch with these notes. And I didn't even remember receiving them.

I thought about my connections in life. I thought about workplace friends who were fired, or had quit due to illness. Who comforted them? Where did they go? Not to me. Not to their former bosses.

Often, it seemed, they were helped by their churches or temples. Members took up collections. They cooked meals. They gave money to pay bills. They did it with love, empathy, and the knowledge that it was part of the supportive under-carriage of a 'sacred community,' like the ones the Reb spoke about, like the one I guess I had once belonged to, even if I didn't realize it.

The plane landed. I collected the papers, wrapped them back in the rubber band, and felt a small grief, like a person who discovers, upon returning from a trip, that something has been left behind and there is no way now to retrieve it.

THANKSGIVING

Fall surrendered quickly in Detroit, and in what seemed like minutes, the trees were bare and the color siphoned out of the city, leaving it a barren and concrete place, under milky skies and early snowfalls. We rolled up the car windows. We took out the heavy coats. Our jobless rate was soaring. People couldn't afford their homes. Some just packed up and walked out, left their whole world behind to bankers or scavengers. It was still November. A long winter lay ahead.

On a Tuesday before Thanksgiving, I came by the I Am My Brother's Keeper Ministry to see firsthand the homeless program it operated. I still wasn't totally at ease with Pastor Henry. Everything about his church was different – at least to me. But what the Reb had said resonated, that you can embrace your own faith's authenticity and still accept that others believe in something else.

Besides, that whole thing about a community – well, Detroit *was* my city. So I put my toe in the water. I helped Henry purchase a blue tarp for his ceiling, which stretched over the leaking section, so at least the sanctuary would not be flooded. Fixing the roof was a much bigger job, maybe eighty thousand dollars, according to a contractor.

'Whoo,' Henry had gushed, when we heard the estimate. Eighty thousand dollars was more than his church had seen in years. I felt badly for him. But that would have to come from some more committed source. A tarp – a toe in the water – was enough from me.

I got out of the car and a freezing wind smacked my cheeks. With the homeless program operating, the side street was populated with men bundled against the cold. A couple of them smoked. I noticed a slight man holding a child, but as I stepped closer I realized that, under the ski cap, it was a woman. I held the door open and she passed in front of me, the child on her shoulder.

Inside, I heard loud grinding hums, like small engines, then a screaming voice. I turned into the catwalk that over-looked the gym. The floor was covered in fold-out tables, and there were maybe eighty homeless men and women sitting around them. They wore old coats and hooded sweat-shirts. A few had parkas; one wore a Detroit Lions jacket.

In the middle of the floor, Henry, in a blue sweat-shirt and a heavy coat, moved between the tables, shifting his weight from one foot to the next.

'I am somebody!' he yelled.

'I am somebody!' the crowd repeated.

'I *am* somebody,' he yelled again.

'I *am* somebody,' they repeated in kind.

'Because God loves me!'

'Because God loves me!'

A few people clapped. Henry exhaled and nodded. One by one, many of the homeless stood up, came into a circle, and held hands. A prayer was recited.

Then, as if on cue, the circle broke and a line formed, leading to the kitchen and something hot to eat.

I tugged on my coat. It felt unusually cold.

'Evenin', Mister Mitch.'

I looked over and saw Cass, the one-legged church elder, sitting on the catwalk, holding a clipboard. The way he greeted me with that lilt in his voice – *'Evenin', Mister Mitch'* – I half-expected him to tip his cap. I had learned that he'd lost the leg a few years ago, to complications from diabetes and heart surgery. Still, he was always so upbeat.

Hi, Cass.

'Pastor's down there.'

Henry looked up, gave a small wave. Cass watched me wave back.

'When you gonna hear *my* story, Mister Mitch?'

You've got a story, too?

'I got a story you need to hear.'

Sounds like it could take a few days.

He laughed. 'Naw, naw. But you oughta hear it. It's important.'

All right, Cass. We'll figure something out.

That seemed to appease him and, thankfully, he dropped the subject. I shivered and pulled my coat tighter.

It's really cold in here, I said.

'They turned off the heat.'

Who?

'Gas company.'

Why?

'Why else? Didn't pay the bill, I suppose.'

The humming noise was overwhelming. We were shouting just to be heard.

What *is* that? I asked.

'Blowers.'

He pointed to several machines that looked like yellow windsocks, pushing warmed air toward the homeless, who waited in line for chili and corn bread.

They really turned your heat off? I said.

'Ye-up.'

But winter's coming.

'That's true,' Cass said, looking down at the crowd. 'Be a lot more people in here soon.'

Thirty minutes later, up in his office, Henry and I sat huddled by a space heater. Someone came in and offered us a paper plate with corn bread.

What happened? I asked.

Henry sighed. 'Turns out we owe thirty-seven thousand dollars to the gas company.'

What?

'I knew we were running behind, but it was small amounts. We always managed to pay something. Then it got cold so quick this fall, and we started heating the sanctuary for services and Bible study. We didn't realize that the hole in the roof—'

Was sucking the heat up?

'Up and out. We just kept heating it more—'

And it kept disappearing out the roof.

'Disappearing.' He nodded. 'That's the word.'

What do you do now?

'Well, we got blowers. At first, they shut off our electricity, too. But I called and begged them to leave us something.'

I couldn't believe it. A church in the cold, in America, in the twenty-first century.

How do you explain that with your faith? I said.

'I ask Jesus that a lot,' Henry said. 'I say, 'Jesus, is there something going on with us?' Is it like the book of Deuteronomy, the twenty-eighth chapter, "You will be cursed in the city and cursed in the country" for living in disobedience?'

And what does Jesus answer you?

'I'm still praying. I say, "God, we need to see you."'

He sighed.

'That's why that tarp you helped with was so

179

important, Mitch. Our people needed a glimmer of hope. Last week it rained and water gushed in the sanctuary; this week it rained, and it didn't. To them, that's a sign.'

I squirmed. I didn't want to be part of a sign. Not in a church. It was just a tarp. A sheet of blue plastic.

Can I ask you something? I said.

'Sure.'

When you were selling drugs, how much money did you have?

He rubbed a hand on the back of his neck. 'Man. Do you know, in one stretch, over a year and a half, I brought in about a half a million dollars?'

And now your gas gets shut off?

'Yeah,' he said, softly. 'Now the gas gets shut off.'

I didn't ask if he missed those days. Looking back, it was cruel enough to have asked the first question.

Later, when the plates had been cleared and the tables folded, Cass called names off the clipboard – 'Everett! . . . DeMarcus!' – and one by one, the homeless men stepped up and took a thin vinyl mattress and a single wool blanket. Side by side, a few feet from one another, they set up for the night. Some carried plastic trash bags with their possessions; others had only the clothes they were wearing. It was bone-cold, and Cass's voice echoed off the gym ceiling. The men were mostly silent, as if this were the moment when it really sank in: no home, no bed, no 'good night' from a wife or a child.

The blowers roared.

An hour later, Cass, his work finished, lifted himself on his crutches and hobbled to the vestibule. The lights in the gym were dimmed. The men were down for the night.

'Remember, next time, I tell you *my* story,' Cass said.

Okay, sure, Cass, I said. My hands were dug into my pockets, and my arms and torso were shivering. I couldn't imagine how these men slept in this cold, except that the alternative was on a rooftop or in an abandoned car.

I was about to go when I realized I had left a notepad up in Henry's office. I climbed the stairs, but the door was locked. I came back down.

On my way out, I took one last peek into the gym. I heard the steady hum of the blowers and saw the shadowy bumps under blankets, some lying still, some tossing slightly. It's hard to express what hit me then, except the thought that every one of those bumps was a man, every man once a child, every child once held by his mother, and now this: a cold gym floor at the bottom of the world.

I wondered how – even if we had been disobedient – this wouldn't break God's heart.

My eye caught a flicker of movement across the way. A large, lonely figure sat in the darkness. Pastor

181

Henry would remain there for several more hours, watching over the homeless like a sentinel, until the overnight guy arrived. Then he would bundle up, go out the side entrance, and walk home.

I had a sudden urge to get to my own warm bed. I pushed through the door and blinked, because it had started to snow.

I walked a mile with Pleasure;
She chatted all the way;
But left me none the wiser
For all she had to say.

I walked a mile with Sorrow,
And ne'er a word said she;
But, oh! The things I learned from
   her,
When Sorrow walked with me.
          ROBERT BROWNING HAMILTON

THE END OF AUTUMN

'**S**omething happened.'

It was the Reb's daughter, Gilah, who had called me on my cell phone, something she was unlikely to do unless there was trouble. The Reb, she said, had suffered a setback, maybe a stroke, maybe a heart attack. His balance was off. He was falling to the right. He couldn't remember names. His speech was confused.

He had gone to the hospital. He'd been there a few days. They were discussing 'options.'

Is he going to be . . . ? I asked.

'We just don't know,' she said.

I hung up and called the airlines.

It was Sunday morning when I arrived at the house. Sarah greeted me. She pointed to the Reb, released from the hospital and now sitting in a recliner near the back of the den.

'All right, just so you know,' she said, her voice lowered, 'he's not so . . .'

I nodded.

'Al?' she announced. 'You have a visitor.'

She said it loudly and slowly enough that I could

tell things had changed. I approached the Reb, and he turned his head. He lifted his chin slightly, pushed up a small smile, and raised one hand, but barely above his chest.

'Ahh,' he expelled.

He was tucked under a blanket. He wore a flannel shirt. A whistle of some sort was around his neck.

I leaned over him. I brushed his cheek with mine.

'Ehh . . . mmm . . . Mitch,' he whispered.

How are you doing? It was a stupid question.

'It's not . . . ,' he began. Then he stopped.

It's not . . . ?

He grimaced.

It's not the *best* day of your life? I said. A lame attempt at humor.

He tried to smile.

'No,' he said. 'I mean to . . . this . . .'

This?

'Where . . . see . . . ah . . .'

I swallowed hard. I felt my eyes tearing up.

The Reb was sitting in the chair.

But the man I knew was gone.

What do you do when you lose a loved one too quickly? When you have no time to prepare before, suddenly, that soul is gone?

Ironically, the man who could best answer that was sitting in front of me.

Because the worst loss you can suffer had already happened to him.

It was 1953, just a few years into his job at the temple. He and Sarah had a growing family: their son, Shalom, who was now five, and their four-year-old twin girls, Orah and Rinah. The first name means light. The second means joy.

In a single night, joy was lost.

Little Rinah, a buoyant child with curly auburn hair, was having trouble breathing. Lying in her bed, she was gasping and wheezing. Sarah heard the noise from her bedroom, went to check, and came running back. 'Al,' she said, hurriedly, 'we have to take her to the hospital.'

As they drove in the darkness, their little girl struggled terribly. Her airways swelled and tightened in her chest. Her lips were turning blue. Nothing like this had ever happened before. The Reb pressed the accelerator.

They rushed into the emergency room of Our Lady of Lourdes Hospital in Camden, New Jersey. The doctors hurried the child into a room. Then came the wait. They stood alone. What could they do? What can anyone do?

In the silent hallway, Albert and Sarah prayed for their child to live.

Hours later, she was dead.

It was a severe asthma attack, the first and last of Rinah's life. Today, most likely, she would have survived. With an inhaler, with instructions, it might not even have been a major incident.

But today is not yesterday, and the Reb could do

nothing but listen to the worst imaginable words –
We *couldn't save her* – told to him by a doctor he
had never met before that night. How could this
happen? She had been perfectly normal earlier in
the day, a playful child, her whole life before her. *We
couldn't save her?* Where is the logic, the order of life?

The next few days were a blur. There was a
funeral, a small coffin. At the grave site, the Reb
said Kaddish, a prayer he had led for so many
others, a prayer which never mentions death, yet
is recited on the anniversary of a death every year
thereafter.

> 'May God's great name be glorified and
> sanctified throughout the world which He
> has created . . .'

A small shovel of dirt was tossed on the grave.
Rinah was buried.
The Reb was thirty-six years old.

'I cursed God,' he'd admitted when we'd spoken
about it. 'I asked Him over and over, "Why her?
What did this little girl do? She was four years
old. She didn't hurt a soul."'
Did you get an answer?
'I still have no answer.'
Did that make you angry?
'For a while, furious.'
Did you feel guilty cursing God – you, of all
people?

'No,' he said. 'Because even in doing so, I was recognizing there was a greater power than me.'

He paused.

'And that is how I began to heal.'

The night the Reb returned to the pulpit, the temple was packed. Some came out of condolence. Some, no doubt, out of curiosity. But privately, most wondered the same thing: 'Now that it's happened to you, what do you have to say?'

The Reb knew this. It was partly why he came back so quickly, the first Friday after the mandatory thirty days of mourning.

And when he rose to his lectern, and when the congregation quieted, he spoke the only way he knew how – from the heart. He admitted that, yes, he had been angry at the Lord. That he'd howled in anguish, that he'd screamed for an answer. That there was nothing in being a Man of God that insulated him from the tears and misery of never being able to hold his little girl again.

And yet, he noted, the very rituals of mourning that he cursed having to do – the prayers, the torn clothing, not shaving, covering the mirrors – had helped him keep a grip on who he was, when he might have otherwise washed away.

'That which I have had to say to others, I must say now to myself,' he admitted, and in so doing, his faith was being tested with the truest test there is: to drink his own elixir, to heal his own broken heart.

He told them how the words of the Kaddish made him think, 'I am part of something here; one day my children will say this very prayer for me just as I am saying it for my daughter.'

His faith soothed him, and while it could not save little Rinah from death, it could make her death more bearable, by reminding him that we are all frail parts of something powerful. His family, he said, had been blessed to have the child on earth, even for a few short years. He would see her again one day. He believed that. And it gave him comfort.

When he finished, nearly everyone was crying.

'Years later,' he told me, 'whenever I would go to someone's home who had lost a family member – a young one, particularly – I would try to be of comfort by remembering what comforted me. Sometimes we would sit quietly. Just sit and maybe hold a hand. Let them talk. Let them cry. And after a while, I could see they felt better.

'And when I'd get outside, I would go like this—'

He touched a finger to his tongue and pointed skyward.

'Chalk one up for you, Rinah,' he said, smiling.

Now, in the back of his house, I was holding the Reb's hand, as he had done for others. I tried to smile. He blinked from behind his glasses.

All right, I said. I'll come back and see you soon. He half-nodded.

'You . . . okay . . . yeah . . . ,' he whispered.

There was little else to do. He was no longer able to speak a full sentence. And with each of my poor attempts at conversation, I felt I was only frustrating him more. He seemed to sense what was happening, and I feared the look on my face would reveal the crushing loss I felt. How was this fair? This wise and eloquent man, who a few weeks earlier had been discoursing on divinity, was now stripped of his most precious faculty; he could no longer teach, he could no longer string together beautiful sentences from that beautiful mind.

He could no longer sing.

He could only squeeze my fingers and move his mouth open and closed.

On the plane ride home, I wrote down some sentences. The eulogy, I feared, was finally coming due.

FROM A SERMON BY THE REB

'**I**f you ask me, and you should, why this wonderful, beautiful child – who had so much to give – had to die, I can't give you a rational answer. I don't know.

'But in a commentary to the Bible, tradition tells us that Adam, our first man, was supposed to have lived longer than any man, a thousand years. He didn't. Our sages, in quest of an answer, related the following:

'Adam begged God to let him see into the future. So the Lord said, "Come with me." He took him through the celestial chambers, where the souls that were to be born awaited their turn. Each soul was a flame. Adam saw some flames burn purely, some barely flicker.

'Then he saw a beautiful flame, clear, strong, golden orange, and healing. Adam said, "Oh Lord, that will be a great human being. When shall it be born?"

'The Lord replied, "I'm sorry, Adam, but that soul, as beautiful as it is, is destined not to be born. It has been preordained that it will commit

191

sin and tarnish itself. I have chosen to spare it the indignity of being besmirched."

'Adam pleaded, "But Lord, man must have someone to teach and guide him. Please, do not deprive my children."

'The Lord gently answered, "The decision has been made. I have no years left to allocate to him."

'Then Adam boldly said, "Lord, what if I am willing to bestow on that soul some of the years of my life?"

'And God answered Adam, saying, "If that is your wish, that I will grant."

'Adam, we are told, died not at 1,000, but at 930 years. And eons later, there was a child born in the town of Bethlehem. He became a ruler over Israel and a sweet singer of songs. After leading his people and inspiring them, he died. And the Bible concludes: "Behold, David the King was buried after having lived for 70 years."

'My friends, when sometimes we are asked why does someone perish, someone so young in age, I can only fall back on the wisdom of our tradition. It is true that David did not live long for his day. But while he lived, David taught, inspired, and left us a great spiritual legacy, including the Book of Psalms. One of those Psalms, the twenty-third, is read sometimes at funerals.

'The Lord is my shepherd; I shall not want.
He maketh me to lie down in green pastures:

He leadeth me beside the still waters.
He restoreth my soul . . .

'Is it not better to have known Rinah, my daughter, for four years, than not to have known her at all?'

WINTER

Then some people came, bringing a paralyzed man, carried by four of them. And when they could not bring him to Jesus because of the crowd, they made a hole in the roof.

MARK 2:3–4

WINTER SOLSTICE

On a Sunday morning, with the snow whipping sideways, I pulled open the church's large front door and stepped into the vestibule. The sanctuary was freezing – and empty. The roof hole was above me. I could hear the wind whipping the blue tarp. An organ sound was coming from somewhere, but there was no one around.

'*Psst.*'

I turned to see the thin man with the high forehead, motioning me to another door on the side. I walked in and did a double take.

Here was some kind of makeshift mini-sanctuary, just two short pews wide, with a side 'wall' of plastic sheeting staple-gunned into wooden two-by-fours. It was like a fort that kids make in the attic. The plastic wrapped overhead as well, creating a low ceiling.

Apparently, with no heat to fight the cold, the church had been forced to build a plastic tent inside its own sanctuary. Congregants huddled in the limited seating. The small space made it less frigid, although people still kept their coats on.

And this was where Pastor Henry Covington now conducted his Sunday service. Instead of a grand altar, he had a small lectern. Instead of the soaring pipe organ behind him, there was a black-and-white banner nailed on the wall.

'We are grateful to you, God,' Henry was saying as I slid into a back row. 'God of hope . . . we give you thanks and praise . . . in Jesus's name, amen.'

I glanced around. Between the roof hole, the heat being shut off, and now a plastic prayer tent, you wondered how long before the church withered out of existence altogether.

Henry's sermon that day had to do with judging people by their past. He began by lamenting how hard it is to shake a habit – especially an addiction.

'I know how it is,' he bellowed. 'I know what it's like when you done swore, 'I'll never do this again . . . next time I get my money, I'm gonna do this and I'm gonna do that,' and you go home and you promise your loved ones, "I messed up, but I'm gonna get back"—'

'*Amen!*'

'And then you get some money, and all those promises – out the window.'

'*Way-ell!*'

'You're so sick and tired of being sick and tired—'

'*Sick and tired!*'

'But there comes a time when you have to admit to God, this stuff is stronger than me – it's stronger than the rehab program – it's stronger than the pastor at the church . . . I need you, Lord . . . I need you, Jesus . . .'

He started clapping.

'But you gotta be like Smokey Robinson . . .'

He burst into song. He did two lines from 'You Really Got a Hold on Me.'

Then back to preaching.

'And maybe you make it to the supermarket and buy some groceries, then someone comes up to you and you get weak . . . and all the groceries that you bought for seventy dollars, you'll give 'em away for twenty—'

'Fifteen!'

'Yes, sir . . . fifteen . . . that's right, if you on a hard enough mission to get high . . . I'm tellin' you, I know what it's like to be in, and I know what it's like to be out.'

'Amen!'

'But we gotta fight this thing. And it's not good enough for just *you* to get clean. If someone else is trying, you gotta believe in them too—'

'Preach it, Pastor!'

'In the Book of Acts, we read that Paul – after his conversion – people distrusted him because he used to persecute the church, but now he praised it. "*Is this the same guy?* Can't be! Nuh-uh." . . . It's amazing how folks can't see you, 'cause they want to keep you in that past. Some of our greatest problems in ministering to people is that they knew us back before we came to the Lord—'

199

'Yes it is!'

'The same thing with Paul . . . They saw him . . . they couldn't believe that this man's from Jesus, because they looked at his past—'

'That's right!'

'They just looked at his past. And when we're still looking at ourselves through our past, we're not seeing what God has done. What He *can* do! We're not seeing the little things that happen in our lives—'

'Tell it now.'

'When people tell me that I'm good, my response is, "I'm trying." But there's some people that know me from back when – anytime I make that trip to New York – and when they hear I'm the pastor of a church, all of a sudden, it's like "I know you gettin' paid, boy. I *know* you gettin' paid. I *know* you."'

He paused. His voice lowered.

'No, I say. You *knew* me. You knew that person, but you don't know the person that I'm trying to become.'

Sitting in the back, I felt a shiver of embarrassment. The truth was, I had struggled with similar thoughts about Henry. I'd wondered if, back among his New York world, he'd laugh and say, 'Yeah, I got a whole new thing going on.'

Instead, here he was, preaching in a plastic tent.

'You are *not* your past!' he told his congregation.

Did you ever hear a sermon that felt as if it were being screamed into your ear alone? When that happens, it usually has more to do with you than the preacher.

DECEMBER

GOOD AND EVIL

After all his years of dogged survival, the Reb, I believed, could beat back any illness; he just might not beat them all.

The attack that had left him slumped in a chair, confused and mumbling, proved not to be a stroke at all, but rather a tragic consequence of his multiple afflictions. In the stir of doctors and prescriptions, the Reb's Dilantin medication – taken, ironically, to control seizures – had been inadvertently increased to levels that pummeled him. Toxic levels.

Simply put, pills had turned the Reb into a human scarecrow.

When the problem was finally discovered – after several terrible months – dosages were quickly adjusted, and he was, in a matter of days, brought out of his crippling stupor.

I first heard about this in a phone call with Gilah and a subsequent one with Sarah.

'It's amazing . . . ,' they said. 'It's remarkable . . .'

There was a buoyancy in their voices I hadn't heard in months, as if an unexpected summer had arrived in their backyard. And when I caught a plane to the East Coast and entered the house myself, and got my first glimpse of the Reb in his office – well, I wish I could describe the feeling. I have read stories about coma patients who suddenly, after years, awaken and ask for a piece of chocolate cake, while loved ones stare in dropped-jaw disbelief. Maybe it was like that.

All I know is that he turned in his chair, wearing one of those vests with all the pockets, and he held out his bony arms, and he smiled in that excited, crinkle-eyed way that seemed to emit sunlight, and he crowed, 'Hellooo, stranger' – and I honestly thought I had seen someone return from the dead.

What was it like? I asked him, when we'd had a chance to settle.

'A fog,' he said. 'Like a dark hole. I was here, but somehow I wasn't here.'

Did you think it was . . . you know . . .

'The end?'

Yeah.

'At times.'

And what were you thinking at those times?

'I was thinking mostly about my family. I wanted to calm them. But I felt helpless to do so.'

You scared the heck out of me – us, I said.

'I am sorry about that.'

No. I mean. It's not your fault.

'Mitch, I have been asking myself why this happened,' he said, rubbing his chin. 'Why I have been . . . *spared,* so to speak. After all, another couple of whatchamacallits . . .'

Milligrams?

'That's it. And I could've been kaput.'

Aren't you furious?

He shrugged. 'Look. I'm not happy, if that's what you're asking. But I must believe the doctors were doing their best.'

I couldn't believe his tolerance. Most people would have been at a lawyer's office. I guess the Reb felt if there was a reason for his rescue, it wasn't to file lawsuits.

'Maybe I have a little more to give,' he said.

Or get.

'When you give, you get,' he said.

I walked right into that one.

Now, I knew the Reb believed that corny line. He truly was happiest when he could help someone. But I assumed a Man of God had no choice. His religion obliged him toward what Lincoln called 'the better angels of our nature.'

On the other hand, Napoleon once dismissed religion as 'what keeps the poor from murdering the rich.' Meaning, without the fear of God – or literally the hell we might have to pay – the rest of us would just take what we wanted.

The news headlines certainly endorsed that idea. In recent months, there had been terrorist train blasts in India, greedy executives sentenced in the Enron fraud case, a truck driver who'd shot five girls in an Amish schoolhouse, and a California congressman sent to jail for taking millions in bribes while living on a yacht.

Do you think it's true, I asked the Reb that day, that our nature is evil?

'No,' he said. 'I believe there is goodness in man.'

So we *do* have better angels?

'Deep down, yes.'

Then why do we do so many bad things?

He sighed. 'Because one thing God gave us – and I'm afraid it's at times a little too much – is free will. Freedom to choose. I believe he gave us everything needed to build a beautiful world, if we choose wisely.

'But we can also choose badly. And we can mess things up something awful.'

Can man change between good and evil?

The Reb nodded slowly. 'In both directions.'

Human nature is a question we've grappled with for centuries. If a child were raised alone, separate from society, media, social dynamics, would that child grow up kind and open-hearted? Or would it be feral and bloodthirsty, looking out solely for its own survival?

We'll never know. We are not raised by wolves. But clearly, we wrestle with conflicting urges. Christianity believes Satan tempts us with evil. Hindus see evil as a challenge to life's balance. Judaism refers to a man's righteous inclination versus his evil inclination as two warring spirits;

the evil spirit can, at first, be as flimsy as a cobweb, but if allowed to grow, it becomes thick as a cart rope.

The Reb once did a sermon on how the same things in life can be good or evil, depending on what, with free will, we do with them. Speech can bless or curse. Money can save or destroy. Science can heal or kill. Even nature can work for you or against you: fire can warm or burn; water can sustain life or flood it away.

'But nowhere in the story of Creation,' the Reb said, 'do we read the word "bad." God did not create bad things.'

So God leaves it to us?

'He leaves it to us,' he replied. 'Now, I do believe there are times when God clenches his fist and says, "Ooh, don't do it, you're gonna get yourself into trouble." And you might say, well, why doesn't God jump in? Why doesn't he eliminate the negative and accentuate the positive?

'Because, from the beginning, God said, "I'm gonna put this world into your hands. If I run everything, then that's not you." So we were created with a piece of divinity inside us, but with this thing called free will, and I think God watches us every day, lovingly, praying we will make the right choices.'

Do you really think God prays? I asked.

'I think prayer and God,' he said, 'are intertwined.'

I stared at him for a moment, marveling at the way he was speaking, analyzing, making jokes. Just weeks ago, hands were being wrung for him, tears were being cried. Now this. His daughter called it a miracle. Maybe it was. I was just relieved that he was better – and that his eulogy could wait.

We heard a honk. The taxi had arrived.

'So, anyhow' he said, wrapping up, 'that is the story of my recent life.'

I stood and gave him a hug, a little tighter than usual.

No more scares, okay?'

'Ah,' he laughed, jerking a thumb skyward. 'You'll have to take that up with my boss.'

LIFE OF CASS

*T*he story of my recent life. I like that phrase. It makes more sense than the *story of my life*, because we get so many lives between birth and death. A life to be a child. A life to come of age. A life to wander, to settle, to fall in love, to parent, to test our promise, to realize our mortality – and, in some lucky cases, to do something after that realization.

The Reb had achieved that.

And so had someone else.

Not Henry – although he certainly lived many lives.

But I refer here to his trusty elder, the man with one leg, who nudged and cajoled me until finally, on a cold night, in a plastic-covered section of the church, he said, in a scratchy voice, 'Mister Mitch, I got to share this with you . . .'

Anthony 'Cass' Castelow, it turned out, did have an eye-popping tale: he'd been a star athlete in a big family, gone to the army, come home, become a local drug dealer.

'But okay, now. Here's what I *really* need to tell you . . .'

And this was the story of his recent life.

'Eighteen years ago – back when I had both my legs – I was stabbed in the stomach in a place called Sweetheart's Bar. I was selling drugs outa there. Two guys came in, and one guy grabbed me from behind and the other guy took the drugs and stabbed me. I nearly died in the hospital. I was gurgling blood. Doctors said I'd be lucky to live through the night. But when I got out, I went back to drugs again.

'Not long after that, the drugs got me sent to prison. Three years. I became a Muslim in there, because the Muslims were clean, they took care of their bodies, and a guy named Usur showed me how to pray, you know, five times a day, on the prayer mats, do the *salahs*, say "Alahu Akbar."

'But this guy, Usur, at the end of it all, he'd whisper, "In Jesus's name, amen." I pulled him to the side one day and he says. "Listen, man, I'm a Muslim in here, but my family out there, they're Christian. I don't know if it's Allah or Jesus Christ after this life. I'm just trying to get in, you understand me? 'Cause I ain't never going home, Cass. Do you understand that I'm gonna *die* in here?"

'Well, I left prison and that kinda messed me up. I drifted away from anything with God and I got back into drugs – crack, pills, weed. Lost all my money. With no place to go, I went back to the Jeffries Projects, where I grew up, and which was abandoned now and being torn down. I kicked in the back door of a unit and slept in there.

'And that was the first night I called myself homeless.'

I nodded along as Cass spoke, still not sure where he was going with this. His hat was pulled over his ears and his glasses and graying beard gave him an almost artsy look, like an aged jazz musician, but his old brown jacket and his amputated leg told a truer tale. When he spoke, his few remaining teeth poked from his gums like tiny yellowed fence posts.

He was determined to get through this story, so I rubbed my hands to keep warm and said, 'Go on, Cass.' Smoke came from my mouth, that's how cold it was in the church.

'All right, Mister Mitch, now here's the thing: I almost died a couple times in those projects. Once, I came back at night and as soon as I walked in, someone whacked me over the head with a gun and cracked my skull open. I never did find out why. But they left me there for dead, bleeding, with my pants pulled down and my pockets turned out.'

Cass leaned over and pulled off his hat. There was a three-inch scar on his head.

'See that?'

He pulled his hat back on.

'Every night in that life, you would either be getting high or drunk or something to try and deal with the reality that you didn't have no place to go. I'd make money all kinds of little ways. Take out garbage for a bar. Panhandle. And of course, I'd just steal. The hockey team and the baseball team, when they was playing, you could always sneak down there and steal one of them orange things and wave people's cars in if you look decent enough. You say, 'Park right here.' Then you run with their money back to the projects and get high.'

I shook my head. With all the hockey and baseball games I'd gone to, I might have handed Cass a few bills myself.

'I was homeless pretty near five years,' he said. 'Five *years*. Sleeping here or there in them abandoned projects. There was a winter night in the rain where I almost froze to death at a bus stop, my stupid behind out there with no place to go. And I was so hungry and so thin, my stomach was touching my back.

'I had two pairs of pants, and they was both on me. I had three shirts, and all three of 'em was on me. I had one gray coat, and it was my pillow, my cover, everything. And I had a pair of Converse gym shoes that had so many holes in it, I loaded up my feet with baking soda to keep them from stinking.'

Where did you get the baking soda?

'Well, come on – we was all out here smoking crack. That's what you cook it with. *Everyone* got baking soda!'

I looked down, feeling stupid.

'And then I heard about this man from New York, Covington. He drove around in this old limo, coming through the neighborhood. He was from a church, so we called him Rebbey Reb.'

Rebbey what? I said.

'Reb.'

Cass leaned forward, squinting, as if everything to this point had been a prelude.

'Reb come around every day with food on top of that car – on the hood, in the trunk. Vegetables. Milk. Juice. Meats. Anybody who was hungry could have some. Once he stopped that car, there'd be like forty or fifty people in a line.

'He didn't ask for nothing. Most he'd do was, at the end, he'd say, "Remember, Jesus loves you." When you homeless, you don't wanna hear much of that, 'cause it's like, when you get through talking about Jesus, I gotta go back to living in this empty building, you know?

'After a while, Pastor got deliveries from these food bank organizations and he'd serve them out the side of his house in an empty field. A few of us made this grill next to his place and we'd heat the food up. People would come from blocks away, they'd bring a bowl, maybe a spoon if they got one – I seen people with plastic bags scooping up food and eating with their hands.

'And Pastor would have a little service right there against his house. Say thanks to God.'

Wait. Outside? Against his house?

'That's what I'm saying. So pretty soon, we're liking this guy. We see him coming, we say, "Here come Rebbey Reb. Hide the dope! Hide the liquor!" And he'd give us a little money to help him unload the food trucks – turkeys, bread, juice. Me and a guy had our own unloading system: one for the church, two for us. We'd throw ours out in the bushes, then come back later and pick it up.

'Eventually, Pastor come to me and say, "You got enough to eat, Cass? Take what you need." He knew what I was doing.

'I felt ashamed.'

'One night in the projects, I had just gotten high and I hear Pastor call my name. I'm embarrassed to come out. My eyes are big as saucers. He asks if I can do some landscaping around his grass the next day. And I said, sure, yeah. And he gives me ten dollars and says meet me tomorrow. When he left, all I wanted to do was run upstairs and buy more dope and get high again. But I didn't want to spend this man's money that way. So I ran across the street and bought lunch meat, crackers – anything so I don't spend it on drugs.

'That night, this guy who's staying where I'm staying, while I'm sleeping, he steals the pipes from under the sink – steals 'em for the copper, so he can sell 'em. And he takes off, and all the water starts running in. I wake up on the floor and the place is flooded. I'm washing away.

'My only clothes is all ruined now, and I go to Pastor's house and I say, "Sorry, I ain't gonna be able to work for you. I'm all soaked." And I'm telling him how mad I am at this guy, and he says, "Cass, don't worry. Sometimes people got it worse than you do."

'And he sends me over to the church, and he says, "Go upstairs, we got some bags of clothes, just pick out what you want.' And I get some clothes – Mitch, it's the first time I got clean underwear in I don't know how long. Clean socks. A shirt. I go back to his place and he says, "Where are you gonna stay now, Cass?"

'And I say, "Don't know. My place is all flooded." And he goes in, talks with his wife, and he comes out and says, "Why don't you stay here with us?"

'Now I'm shocked. I mean, I did a little work for this man. I stole food from him. And now he's opening his home?

'He said, "You wanna think about it?" And I'm like, "What's there to think about? I'm homeless."'

Henry never told me any of this, I said.

'That's why *I'm* telling you,' Cass said. 'I moved in with his family that night. I stayed there almost a year. A *year*. He let me sleep on the couch in his main room. His family is upstairs, they got little kids, and I'm sayin' to myself, this man don't know me, he don't know what I'm capable of. But he trusts me.'

He shook his head and looked away.

'That kindness saved my life.'

We sat there for a second, quiet and cold. I now knew more than I'd ever figured to know about an elder of the I Am My Brother's Keeper Ministry.

What I still didn't know was why.

And then Cass told me: 'I see the way you watch the Pastor. You here a lot. And maybe he ain't the way you think a pastor should be.

'But I truly believe the Lord has given me a second chance on account of this man. When I die, Jesus will stand in the gap for me and I will be heard and the Lord will say, "I know you." And I believe it's the same for Pastor Covington.'

But Henry's done some bad things in his life, I said.

'I know it,' Cass said. 'I done 'em, too. But it's not me against the other guy. It's God measuring you against *you*.

'Maybe all you get are chances to do good, and what little bad you do ain't much bad at all. But because God has put you in the position where you can always do good, when you do something bad – it's like you let God down.

'And maybe people who only get chances to do bad, always around bad things, like us, when they finally make something good out of it, God's happy.'

He smiled and those stray teeth poked into his lips. And I finally realized why he had so wanted to tell me his story.

It wasn't about him at all.
You really called Henry 'Reb'? I asked.
'Yeah. Why?'
Nothing, I said.

What is there that forgiveness cannot achieve?

VIDURA

SAYING SORRY

It was now a few weeks from Christmas, and I dug my hands into my pockets as I approached the Reb's front door. A pace-maker had been put into his chest a few weeks earlier, and while he'd come through the procedure all right, looking back, I think that was the man's last chip. His health was like a slow leak from a balloon. He had made his ninetieth birthday – joking with his children that until ninety, he was in charge, and after that, they could do what they wanted.

Maybe reaching that milestone was enough. He barely ate anymore – a piece of toast or fruit was a meal – and if he walked up the driveway once or twice, it was major exercise. He still took rides to the temple with Teela, his Hindu health care friend. People there helped him from the car into a wheelchair, and inside he'd greet the kids in the after-school program. At the ShopRite, he used the cart like a walker, gripping it for balance. He chatted with the other shoppers. True to his Depression roots, he'd buy bread and cakes from the 'fifty percent off' section. When Teela rolled

218

her eyes, he'd say, 'It's not that I need it – it's that I *got* it!'

He was a joyous man, a marvelous piece of God's machinery, and it was no fun watching him fall apart.

In his office now, I helped him move boxes. He would try to give me books, saying it broke his heart to leave them behind. I watched him roll from pile to pile, looking and remembering, then putting the stuff down and moving to another pile.

If you could pack for heaven, this was how you'd do it, touching everything, taking nothing.

Is there anyone you need to forgive at this point? I asked him.

'I've forgiven them already,' he said.

Everyone?

'Yes.'

Have they forgiven you?

'I hope. I have asked.'

He looked away.

'You know, we have a tradition. When you go to a funeral, you're supposed to stand by the coffin and ask the deceased to forgive anything you've ever done.'

He made a face.

'Personally, I don't want to wait that long.'

I remember when the Reb made his most public of apologies. It was his last High Holiday sermon as the senior rabbi of the temple.

219

He could have used the occasion to reflect on his accomplishments. Instead he asked forgiveness from his flock. He apologized for not being able to save more marriages, for not visiting the home-bound more frequently, for not easing more pain of parents who had lost a child, for not having money to help widows or families in economic ruin. He apologized to teenagers with whom he didn't spend enough teaching time. He apologized for no longer being able to come to workplaces for brown bag lunch discussions. He even apologized for the sin of not studying every day, as illness and commitments had stolen precious hours.

'For all these, God of forgiveness,' he concluded, 'forgive me, pardon me . . .'

Officially, that was his final 'big' sermon.

'Grant me atonement' were his last three words.

And now the Reb was urging me not to wait.

'Mitch, it does no good to be angry or carry grudges.'

He made a fist. 'It churns you up inside. It does you more harm than the object of your anger.'

So let it go? I asked.

'Or don't let it get started in the first place,' he said. 'You know what I found over the years? When I had a disagreement with someone, and they came to talk to me, I always began by saying, 'I've thought about it. And in some ways maybe you're right.'

'Now, I didn't always believe that. But it made things easier. Right from the start, they relaxed. A negotiation could take place. I took a volatile situation and, what's the word . . . ?'

Defused it?

'Defused it. We need to do that. Especially with family.

'You know, in our tradition, we ask forgiveness from everyone – even casual acquaintances. But with those we are closest with – wives, children, parents – we too often let things linger. Don't wait, Mitch. It's such a waste.'

He told me a story. A man buried his wife. At the gravesite he stood by the Reb, tears falling down his face.

'I loved her,' he whispered.

The Reb nodded.

'I mean . . . I really loved her.'

The man broke down.

'And . . . I almost told her once.'

The Reb looked at me sadly.

'Nothing haunts like the things we don't say.'

Later that day, I asked the Reb to forgive me for anything I might have ever said or done that hurt him. He smiled and said that while he couldn't think of anything, he would 'consider all such matters addressed.'

Well, I joked, I'm glad we got that over with.

'You're in the clear.'

Timing is everything.

'That's right. Which is why our sages tell us to repent exactly one day before we die.'

But how do you know it's the day before you die? I asked.

He raised his eyebrows.

'Exactly.'

I will give you a new heart and put a new spirit in you; I will remove from you your heart of stone and give you a heart of flesh.

EZEKIEL 36:26

THE MOMENT OF TRUTH

It was Christmas week in Detroit, but there seemed to be more 'For Sale' signs on houses than blinking lights. Folks were not shopping much. Kids were being warned to expect less from Santa. The Depression of our age was unfolding and we sensed it; we wore it on our faces.

Down on Trumbull, Pastor Henry's church sat cloaked in darkness – they couldn't afford outside lighting – and unless you pulled open the side door, you might not even know the building was occupied. In all my time there, I never saw the place fully illuminated. 'Dim' was pretty much the word for inside, as if the electricity were as old as the walls.

That night with Cass had shown me another way of unraveling Henry – talking to his congregants.

A fellow named Dan, for example, one of the church's few white members, told me that, years earlier, he had been alcoholic and homeless, sleeping nights on a handball court on Detroit's Belle Isle. He would drink a fifth of liquor and up to twelve beers a day, pass out, wake up, and start drinking again. One chilly night he came to the church, but it was closed. Henry, sitting in his car, saw Dan walking away and called him over, then asked if he needed a place to stay.

'He didn't know me from a hill of beans,' Dan told me. 'I could have been Jack the Ripper.' Eventually, Dan got sober by staying thirty straight days in the church.

Another congregant, a short, energetic woman named Shirley, recalled twenty or thirty kids sleeping at Henry's small house on Friday nights or Saturday afternoons. He called the group the 'Peace Posse.' He taught them to cook, he played games, but mostly he made them feel safe. Henry so inspired Shirley that she became a church elder.

A man named Freddie showed me the private room with the wooden bed frame that he lived in on the church's third floor. He said Henry offered it to him when he was out on the streets. A lady named Luanne noted that Henry never charged for a funeral or a wedding. 'The Lord will pay us back,' he would say.

And then there was Marlene, a handsome woman with sad, almond eyes, who told me a brutal tale of drug addiction and violence, culminating in a confrontation with the man she was living with: he yanked her and her two-year-old son out of bed, beat her, and pushed them down a flight of stairs. They landed on an old board with nails in it, and her son gashed his forehead.

The man refused to let them go to a hospital. He literally held them captive while they bled.

Two days later, he finally left the house, and Marlene grabbed her son and ran – with only the clothes they were wearing. At the police station, an officer called Henry, who spoke to Marlene over the phone. He sounded so concerned and soothing that she asked the police to take her to his church, even though she'd never met him. Henry gave Marlene and her son a hot meal and a place to sleep – and she'd been coming to his ministry ever since.

I thought about how churches and synagogues usually build memberships. Some run schools. Some host social events. Some offer singles nights, lecture series, carnivals, and sign-up drives. Annual dues are part of the equation.

At I Am My Brother's Keeper, there were no dues, no drives, no singles nights. Membership grew the old-fashioned way: a desperate need for God.

Still, none of this helped Henry with his heating problems or his bills. His Sunday services continued inside a plastic tent. The homeless nights were still noisy with hot air blowers, and the men kept their coats on when they lay down to sleep. Early winter continued its attack, and the snow piled up on the church's front steps.

Although I tended to stay away from religious themes in my newspaper writing, I felt a need to expose these conditions to the readership of the

Detroit Free Press. I did interviews with a few of the homeless, including a man who was once an excellent baseball player, but who'd lost all ten toes to frostbite after spending the night in an abandoned car.

I filed the stories, but something still nagged at me.

And so one night, just before Christmas, I went to Henry's house. It was down the block from the church. He had mortgaged it for thirty thousand dollars, back when he arrived in Detroit sixteen years ago. It might not be worth that today.

The brick facade was old, a front gate was loose, and the empty lot where he'd once served food to the neighborhood was matted with snow, ice, and mud. The shed where they stored the food was still there, with netting to protect it from birds.

Henry sat on a small couch in his front room — where Cass once spent a year. He was suffering a head cold and he coughed several times. His place was tidy but poor, the paint was peeling, and the ceiling in the kitchen had partially collapsed. He seemed more pensive than usual. Maybe it was the holiday. His walls held photos of his children, but it was clear they weren't getting a lot of Christmas presents this year.

In his drug dealing days, if Henry wanted a TV, customers would trade him one for dope. Jewelry? Designer clothes? He didn't even need to leave his house.

I asked if he ever thought, when he entered the ministry, that one day he might be doing better than he was?

'No,' he said. 'I think I was meant to work with the poor.'

Yeah, I joked, but you don't have to *imitate* them.

He looked around at the crumbling house. He drew a deep breath.

'I'm where I'm supposed to be.'

How do you mean?

He lowered his eyes.

Then he said something I will never forget.

'Mitch, I am an awful person. The things I have done in my life, they can never be erased. I have broken every one of the Ten Commandments.'

Come on. Every one?

'When I was younger, in some way, yes, every one.'

Stealing? False witness? Coveting?

'Yes.'

Adultery?

'Umm-hmm.'

Murder?

'I never pulled the trigger, but I was involved enough. I could have stopped things before a life was taken. I didn't. So I was involved in murder.'

He looked away.

'It was a cutthroat business, dog eat dog, the strong preying on the weak. In the lifestyle I was in, people were killed. It happened every day.

'I hate that person I was. I went to prison for a crime I did not do, but I did things out here that I should have gone back for. I was cowardly. I was hard. That may not be who I am now, but it's who I was.'

He sighed. 'It's who I was.'

His chin dropped to his chest. I heard his nasal breathing, in and out.

'I deserve hell,' he whispered. 'The things I've done, God would be justified. God is not mocked. What you sow, you reap.

'That's why I tell my congregation, don't put me on a pedestal. I sermonize about wanting cherries when you're planting lemons, but I've planted many lemons in my life . . .'

His eyes were teary now.

'. . . and I may not have reaped all that harvest.'

I don't understand, I said. If you think you're going to be punished—

'Why still serve God?' He smiled weakly. 'What else can I do? It's like when everyone was turning away, and Jesus asked the apostles, 'Will you go, too?' And Peter said, "Where can I go, Lord?"

'I know what he meant. Where do you go from God? He's everywhere.'

But, Henry, all the good you do here—

'No.' He shook his head. 'You can't work your way into heaven. Anytime you try and justify yourself with works, you disqualify yourself with works. What I do here, every day, for the rest of my life, is only my way of saying, "Lord, regardless of what eternity holds for me, let me give something back to you. I know it don't even no scorecard. But let me make something of my life before I go . . .'"

He exhaled a long weary breath.

"'And then, Lord, I'm at your mercy.'"

It was late and cold and Henry's past was all over the room. After a few silent minutes, I stood and zipped my coat. I wished him the best, and went back out into the snow.

I used to think I knew everything. I was a 'smart person' who 'got things done,' and because of that, the higher I climbed, the more I could look down and scoff at what seemed silly or simple, even religion.

But I realized something as I drove home that night: that I am neither better nor smarter, only luckier. And I should be ashamed of thinking I knew everything, because you can know the whole world and still feel lost in it. So many people are in pain – no matter how smart or accomplished – they cry, they yearn, they hurt. But instead of looking down on things, they look up, which is where I should have been looking, too. Because when the world quiets to the sound of your own breathing, we all want the same things: comfort, love, and a peaceful heart.

Maybe the first half of his life he did worse than most, and maybe the second half he did better. But that night was the last time I questioned how much Henry Covington's past should shadow his future. Scripture says, 'Judge not.' But God had the right to, and Henry lived with that every day. It was enough.

JANUARY

HEAVEN

January arrived and the calendar changed. It was 2008. Before the year was done, there would be a new U.S. President, an economic earthquake, a sinkhole of confidence, and tens of millions unemployed or without homes. Storm clouds were gathering.

Meanwhile, the Reb puttered from room to room in quiet contemplation. Having survived the Great Depression and two world wars, he was no longer thrown by headline events. He kept the outside world at bay by keeping the inside world at hand. He prayed. He chatted with God. He watched the snow out the window. And he cherished the simple rituals of his day: the prayers, the oatmeal with cereal, the grandkids, the car trips with Teela, the phone calls to old congregants.

I was visiting again on a Sunday morning. My parents had made plans to swing by later and take me to lunch before I flew back to Detroit.

Two weeks earlier, on a Saturday night, the temple had held a gathering in the Reb's honor, commemorating his six decades of service. It was like a coming home party.

232

'I tell you,' the Reb said, shaking his head as if in disbelief, 'there were people who hadn't seen one another in years. And when I saw them hugging and kissing like such long lost friends – I cried. I *cried*. To see what we have created together. It is something incredible.'

Incredible? My old temple? That small place of Sabbath mornings and funny holidays and kids hopping out of cars and running into religious school? Incredible? The word seemed too lofty. But when the Reb pushed his hands together, almost prayer-like, and whispered, 'Mitch, don't you see? We have made a *community*,' and I considered his aging face, his slumped shoulders, the sixty years he had devoted tirelessly to teaching, listening, trying to make us better people, well, given the way the world is going, maybe 'incredible' is the right description.

'The way they hugged each other,' he repeated, his eyes far away, 'for me, that is a piece of heaven.'

It was inevitable that the Reb and I would finally speak about the afterlife. No matter what you call it – Paradise, Moksha, Valhalla, Nirvana – the next world is the underpinning of nearly all faiths. And more and more, as his earthly time wound down, the Reb wondered what lay ahead in what he called '*Olam Habah*' – the world to come. In his voice and in his posture, I could sense he was searching for it now, the way you stretch your neck near the top of a hill to see if you can look over.

The Reb's cemetery plot, I learned, was closer to his birthplace in New York, where his mother and father were buried.

His daughter, Rinah, was buried there, too. When the time came, the three generations would be united, at least in the earth and, if his faith held true, somewhere else as well.

Do you think you'll see Rinah again? I asked.

'Yes, I do.'

But she was just a child.

'Up there,' he whispered, 'time doesn't matter.'

The Reb once gave a sermon in which heaven and hell were shown to a man. In hell, people sat around a banquet table, full of exquisite meats and delicacies. But their arms were locked in front of them, unable to partake for eternity.

'This is terrible,' the man said. 'Show me heaven.'

He was taken to another room, which looked remarkably the same. Another banquet table, more meats and delicacies. The souls there also had their arms out in front of them.

The difference was, they were feeding each other.

What do you think? I asked the Reb. Is heaven like that?

'How can I say? I believe there's something. That's enough.'

He ran a finger across his chin. 'But I admit . . .

in some small way, I am excited by dying, because soon I will have the answer to this haunting question.'

Don't say that.

'What?'

About dying.

'Why? It upsets you?'

Well. I mean. Nobody likes to hear that word. I sounded like a child.

'Listen, Mitch . . .' His voice lowered. He crossed his arms over his sweater, which covered another plaid shirt that had no connection to his blue pants. 'I know my passing will be hard on certain people. I know my family, my loved ones – you, I hope – will miss me.'

I would. More than I could tell him.

'Heavenly Father, please,' he melodized, looking up, 'I am a happy man. I have helped develop many things down on earth. I've even developed Mitch here a little . . .'

He pointed at me with a long, aged finger.

'But this one, you see, he's still asking questions. So, Lord, please, give him many more years. That way, when we are reunited, we'll have lots to talk about.'

He smiled impishly.

'Eh?'

Thank you, I said.

'You're welcome,' he said.

He blinked behind his glasses.

Do you really think we'll meet again one day?

'Don't you?'

Well, come on, I said, sheepishly. I doubt I'm going to whatever level you're going to.

'Mitch, why do you say that?'

Because you're a Man of God.

He looked at me gratefully.

'You're a man of God, too,' he whispered. 'Everyone is.'

The doorbell rang, breaking the mood. I heard my parents talking with Sarah in the other room. I gathered up my things. I told the Reb about the Super Bowl in a few weeks – 'Ahhh, the Super Bowl,' he cooed, which was funny, because I doubt he'd ever watched one – and soon my mother and father entered the room and exchanged hellos as I zipped up my bag. Because he couldn't easily rise from the chair, the Reb stayed seated as they spoke.

How funny when life repeats a pattern. This could have been forty years earlier, a Sunday morning, my parents picking me up from religious school, my dad driving, all of us going out to eat. The only difference was that now, instead of running from the Reb, I didn't want to leave.

'Heading to lunch?' he asked.

Yes, I said.

'Good. Family. That's how it should be.'

I gave him a hug. His forearms pressed tightly behind my neck, tighter than I ever remembered.

He found a song.

'*Enjoy* yourselves . . . its laaaa-ter than you think . . .'

I had no idea how right he was.

CHURCH

'Y ou need to come down here and see some-thing.'

Henry's voice on the phone had been excited. I got out of the car and noticed more vehicles than usual on the street, and several people going in and out of the side door – people I had not seen before. Some were black, some were white. All were dressed better than the average visitor.

When I stepped onto the catwalk, Henry saw me, smiled widely, and opened his huge wingspan.

'I gotta show you some love,' he said.

I felt his big, bare arms squeezing in. Then it hit me. He was wearing a T-shirt.

The heat was back on.

'It's like Miami Beach in here!' he yelled.

Apparently embarrassed by the attention of the newspaper columns, the gas company had renewed its service. And a deal was being worked out for the church to more gradually pay off its debt. The new faces coming in and out were people also moved by the story of Henry's church; they had come to cook meals and help serve them. I noticed a full crowd of homeless folks at the tables, men and women alike, and many had their coats off. Without the cacophony of the air blowers, you heard the more pleasant rumble of conversation.

'It's something, isn't it?' Henry said. 'God is good.'

I walked down to the gym floor. I saw the man I had written about who was missing his toes. In the story, I had mentioned that his wife and daughter had left him eight years earlier, contributing to his decline. Apparently, someone saw his photo and made a connection.

'I'm going to see them right now,' the man said.

Who? Your wife?

'And my little girl.'

Right now?

'Yeah. It's been eight years, man.'

He sniffed. I could tell he wanted to say something.

'Thank you,' he finally whispered.

And he took off.

I don't know if any thank-you ever got to me the way that one did.

As I was leaving, I saw Cass on his crutches.

'Mister Mitch,' he chimed.

Things are a little warmer now, huh? I said.

'Yes, sir,' he said. 'Folks down there are pretty happy, too.'

I looked again and saw a line of men and women. At first I assumed it was for food, maybe second helpings; but then I saw a table and some volunteers handing out clothing.

One large man pulled on a winter jacket, then yelled up to Henry, 'Hey, Pastor, ain't you got no triple XL's?'

Henry laughed.

What's going on? I asked.

'Clothing,' Henry said. 'It's been donated.'

I counted several big piles.

That's a good amount of stuff, I said.

Henry looked at Cass. 'He didn't see?'

Next thing I knew, I was following behind the heavy-set pastor and the one-legged elder, wondering why I always seemed to clomp on the heels of the faithful.

Cass found a key. Henry pulled a door open.

'Take a look,' he said.

And there, inside the sanctuary, was bag after bag after bag after bag – of clothing, jackets, shoes, coats, and toys – filling every pew from front to back.

I swallowed a lump. Henry was right. At that moment, it didn't matter what name you used. God is good.

FROM A SERMON BY THE REB, 2000

'Dear friends. I'm dying.
'Don't be upset. I began to die on July 6, 1917. That's the day I was born, and, in council with what our psalmist says, "We who are born, are born to die."

'Now, I heard a little joke that deals with this. A minister was visiting a country church, and he began his sermon with a stirring reminder:

'"Everyone in this parish is going to die!"

'The minister looked around. He noticed a man in the front pew, smiling broadly.

'"Why are you so amused?" he asked.

'"I'm not from this parish,' the man said. 'I'm just visiting my sister for the weekend."'

FEBRUARY

GOODBYE

The car pulled up to the ShopRite. It was the first week in February, snow was on the ground, and the Reb looked out the window. Teela parked, shut the ignition, and asked if he was coming in.

'I'm a little tired,' he said. 'I'll wait here.'

Looking back, that was surely a clue. The Reb adored the supermarket – for him to pass it up, something had to be wrong.

'Can you leave the music on?' he asked Teela.

'Sure,' she said. And while she shopped for milk, bread, and prune juice, the Reb sat alone, in the snowy parking lot, listening to Hindi chants. It would be his last private moments in the outside world.

By the time they got home, he looked sluggish and felt achy. Calls were made. He was taken to the hospital. The nurses there asked him simple questions – his name, his address – all of which he answered. He couldn't remember the exact date, but he knew it was the presidential election primary, and he cracked that if his candidate lost by one vote, 'I'm gonna kill myself.'

★   ★   ★

242

He stayed for tests. His family visited. The next night, his youngest daughter, Gilah, was with him in the room. She had tickets to Israel and was worried about leaving.

'I don't think I should go,' she said.

'Go,' he said. 'I won't do anything without you.'

His eyes were closing. Gilah called the nurse. She asked if her father could get his medication early, so he could sleep.

'Gil . . . ,' the Reb mumbled.

She took his hand.

'Remember the memories.'

'Okay,' Gilah said, crying, 'now I'm definitely not going.'

'You go,' he said. 'You can remember over there, too.'

They sat for a while, father and daughter. Finally, Gilah rose and reluctantly kissed him goodnight. The nurse gave him his pills. On her way out, he whispered after her.

'Please . . . if you turn off the lights, could you stop by once in a while and remember I'm here?'

The nurse smiled.

'Of course. We can't forget the singing rabbi.'

The next morning, shortly after sunrise, the Reb was awakened for a sponge bath. It was quiet and early. The nurse bathed him gently, and he was singing and humming to her, alive with the day.

Then his head slumped and his music stopped forever.

*I*t is summer and we are sitting in his office. I ask him why he thinks he became a rabbi. He counts on his fingers.

'Number one, I always liked people.

'Number two, I love gentleness.

'Number three, I have patience.

'Number four, I love teaching.

'Number five, I am determined in my faith.

'Number six, it connects me to my past.

'Number seven – and lastly – it allows me to fulfill the message of our tradition: to live good, to do good, and to be blessed.'

I didn't hear God in there.

He smiles.

'God was there before number one.'

THE EULOGY

The seats were all taken. The sanctuary was full. There were mumbled greetings and tear-filled hugs, but people avoided looking at the pulpit. You face front for any funeral service, but you are rarely staring at the empty space of the deceased. *He used to sit in that chair . . . He used to stand by that lectern . . .*

The Reb had lived a few days beyond his massive stroke, in a peaceful coma, long enough for his wife, children, and grandchildren to get there and whisper their good-byes. I had done the same, touching his thick white hair, hugging my face to his, promising he would not die the second death, he would not be forgotten, not as long as I had a breath in me. In eight years, I had never cried in front of the Reb.

When I finally did, he couldn't see me.

I went home and waited for the phone call. I did not start on his eulogy. It felt wrong to do so while he was still alive. I had tapes and notes and photos and pads; I had texts and sermons and newspaper clippings; I had an Arabic schoolbook with family photos.

245

When the call finally came, I began to write. And I never looked at any of that stuff.

Now, inside my jacket, I felt the typed pages, his last request of me, folded in my pocket. Nearly eight years had passed in what I once thought would be a two- or three-week journey. I had used up most of my forties. I looked older in the mirror. I tried to remember the night this all started.

Will you do my eulogy?

It felt like a different life.

With a quiet grace, his service began, the first service in sixty years of this congregation that Albert Lewis could not lead or join. After a few minutes, after a few prayers, the current rabbi, Steven Lindemann – whom the Reb had graciously welcomed as his replacement – spoke lovingly and beautifully of his predecessor. He used the haunting phrase, 'Alas for what has been lost.'

Then the sanctuary quieted. It was my turn.

I climbed the carpeted steps and passed the casket of the man who had raised me in his house of prayer and in his faith – his beautiful faith – and my breath came so sporadically, I thought I might have to stop just to find it.

I stood where he used to stand.

I leaned forward.

And this is what I said.

Dear Rabbi—

Well, you did it. You finally managed to get us all here when it wasn't the High Holidays.

I guess, deep down, I knew this day would come. But standing here now, it all feels backwards. I should be down there. You should be up here. This is where you belong. This is where we always looked for you, to lead us, to enlighten us, to sing to us, to quiz us, to tell us everything from Jewish law to what page we were on.

There was, in the construction of the universe, us down here, God up there, and you in between. When God seemed too intimidating to face, we could first come to you. It was like befriending the secretary outside the boss's office.

But where do we look for you now?

Eight years ago, you came to me after a speech I gave, and you said you had a favor to ask. The favor was this: would I speak at your funeral? I was stunned. To this day, I don't know why me.

But once you asked, I knew two things: I could never say no. And I needed to get to know you better, not as a cleric, but as a human being. So we began to visit. In your office, in your home, an hour here, two hours there.

One week turned to a month. One month turned to a year. Eight years later, I sometimes wonder if the whole thing wasn't some clever rabbi trick to lure me into an adult education course. You laughed and cried in our meetings; we debated and postulated big ideas and small ones. I learned that, in addition to robes, you sometimes wore sandals with black socks – not a great look – and Bermuda shorts, and plaid shirts and down vests. I learned that you were a pack rat of letters, articles, crayon drawings, and old 'Temple Talk' newsletters. Some people collect cars or clothes. You never met a good idea that couldn't be filed.

I once told you I was not like you, that I was not a man of God. You interrupted and said, 'You are a man of God.' You told me I would find something to say when this day came.

But it is here, and you are gone.

And this pulpit seems as empty as a desert.

But all right, here are your basics, for any good eulogy should contain the basics. You were born in New York during the First World War, your family endured terrible poverty, and your father once rode the rails to Alaska – and never broke the laws of keeping kosher. Your grandfather and father-in-law were rabbis – you had rabbis all over your family tree – and yet you wanted to be a history teacher. You loved to teach. In time, you tried the rabbinate. And you failed. But a great Jewish scholar said

248

two words you would later invoke many times with many of us: 'try again.'

And you did. Thank God you did.

When you were ordained, the popular thing was to go west, to California. There were rich and growing synagogues there. Instead, you went two hours down the New Jersey Turnpike, to a congregation on its last legs, operating out of a converted house. You did it because, like Jimmy Stewart in It's a Wonderful Life, you felt an obligation to stay near your family. And like Stewart's character, you never did get away from this place. Instead, you built this temple. Some would say you carried it on your back.

Under your loving care, it grew from that converted house to a blossoming synagogue pitched between two churches – not exactly the easiest geography. But you always made the best peace. When a Catholic priest from across the street insulted one of our members, you demanded he apologize. When he did, you accepted, as his penance, a gesture. You waited until the Catholic schoolkids were in recess, playing in the schoolyard, then you and the priest strolled around the perimeter, arm in arm, showing that different faiths can indeed walk side by side, in harmony.

You stood up for us that way, you stood tall for us, you built our membership, you built our school, you built a sacred community, you built until we burst at the seams. You led marches and excursions. You made house calls. Endless house calls.

You were a clergyman of the people, never above the people, and people clamored to hear you, stuffing in for your sermons as if to miss them would be a sin in itself. I know you always hated how there was a noisy rush to the exits after you finished. But Reb, think of how many synagogues in which that happens before the sermon starts!

After rabbing through six different decades, you finally stepped down from the pulpit, and instead of moving to Florida, as many do, you simply took a seat in the back row of this sanctuary. It was a humble act, but you could no more move to the back row than the soul could move to the back of the body.

This is your house, Reb. You are in the rafters, the floorboards, the walls, the lights. You are in every echo through every hallway. We hear you now. I hear you still.

How can I – how can any of us – let you go? You are woven through us, from birth to death. You educated us, married us, comforted us. You stood at our mileposts, our weddings, our funerals. You gave us courage when tragedy struck, and when we howled at God, you stirred the embers of our faith and reminded us, as a respected man once said, that the only whole heart is a broken heart.

Look at all the broken hearts here today. Look at all the faces in this sanctuary. My whole life, I had one rabbi. Your whole life, you had one congregation. How do we say good-bye to you without saying good-bye to a piece of ourselves?

Where do we look for you now?

Remember, Reb, when you told me about your childhood neighborhood in the Bronx, such a crowded, tight-knit community that when you nudged a cart, hoping an apple would fall off, a neighbor five floors up yelled out the window, 'Albert, that's forbidden.' You lived with the wagging finger of God on every fire escape.

Well, you were our finger, wagging out the window. How much good have you done simply by the bad we have not? Many of us here have moved away, taken new addresses, new jobs, new climates, but in our minds, we kept the same old rabbi. We could look out our windows and still see your face, still hear your voice on the wind.

But where do we look for you now?

In our last visits, You spoke often about dying, about what comes next. You would cock your head and sing, 'Nu, Lord above, if you want to take me, maybe take me without too much paaaain.'

By the way, Reb, about the singing. What gives? Walt Whitman sang the body electric. Billie Holiday sang the blues. You sang . . . everything. You could sing the phone book. I would call and say how are you feeling, and you'd answer, 'The old gray rabbi, ain't what he used to be . . .'

I teased you about it, but I loved it, I think we all loved it, and it comes as no surprise that you were singing to a nurse last week, preparing for a bath, when the final blow took you from us. I like to think the Lord so enjoyed hearing one of his children joyous – joyous enough to sing in a hospital – that he chose that moment, you in mid-hum, to bring you to him.

So now you are with God. That I believe. You told me your biggest wish, after you died, would be that somehow you could speak to us here, inform us that you had landed, safe and sound. Even in your demise, you were looking for one more sermon.

But you knew there is a maddening yet majestic reason you cannot speak to us today, because if you could, we might not need faith. And faith is what you were all about. You were the salesman that you cited so often in a Yiddish proverb, coming back each day, knocking on the door, offering your wares with a smile, until one day, the customer gets so fed up with your persistence, he spits in your face. And you take out a handkerchief you wipe the spit away, and you smile again and say, 'It must be raining.'

There are handkerchiefs here today, Reb, but it is not because of rain. It's because some of us can't bear to let you go. Some of us want to apologize for all the times we said, through our actions, 'Go away,' for all the times we spit in the face of our faith.

I didn't want to eulogize you. I was afraid. I felt a congregant could never eulogize his leader. But I realize now that thousands of congregants will eulogize you today, in their car rides home, over the dinner table. A eulogy is no more than a summation of memories, and we will never forget you, because we cannot forget you, because we will miss you every day. To imagine a world without you in it is to imagine a world with a little less God in it, and yet, because God is not a diminishing resource, I cannot believe that.

Instead, I have to believe that you have melted back into His glory, your soul is like a returned favor, you are a star in his sky and a warm feeling in our hearts. We believe that you are with your forefathers, with your daughter, with your past, and at peace.

May God keep you; may he sing to you, and you to him.

Where do we look for you now, Reb?

We look where you have been trying – good, sweet Man of God – to get us to look all along.

We look up.

... THE THINGS WE LEAVE BEHIND

Emptiness is not tangible, but after the Reb died, I swear I could touch it, especially on Sundays when I used to make that train trip from New York. Over time, I filled that slot closer to home, with visits to Pastor Henry and the church on Trumbull. I got to know members of his congregation. I enjoyed his sermons. And although I was comfortable, more than ever, with my own faith, Henry laughingly dubbed me 'the first official Jewish member of the congregation.' I came to the homeless nights and wrote more stories about them. People were moved. Some sent money – five dollars, ten dollars. One man drove an hour down a Michigan highway, walked in, looked around, seemed to choke up, then handed over a check for a thousand dollars and left.

Henry opened a bank account for repairs. Volunteers came down to serve food. One Sunday, a large suburban church, the Northville Christian Assembly, invited Henry out to the suburbs to speak. I went to watch him. He wore a long black robe and a wireless microphone. The scripture he chose was flashed up on two giant video screens as he read along. The lighting was perfect, the ceiling solid and dry, the sound was concert quality – there was even a huge grand piano on the stage – and the audience was almost entirely white and middle-class. But Henry was Henry, and before long, he was moving around, exhorting the crowd to earn interest on their talents, as Jesus had once urged in a parable. He told them not to be afraid of coming to his church in Detroit, to use their talents there. 'If you're looking for the miracles God can do with a life,' he said, 'you're looking at one.'

When he finished, everyone stood and clapped. Henry stepped back and humbly lowered his head.

I thought about his dilapidated church downtown. And I realized that, in some ways, we all have a hole in our roof, a gap through which tears fall and bad events blow like harsh wind. We feel vulnerable; we worry about what storm will strike next.

But seeing Henry that day, being cheered by all those new faces, I believe, as the Reb once told me, that, with a little faith, people can fix things, and they truly can change, because at that moment, you could not believe otherwise.

And so, although it is cold as I write this, with snow packed atop the blue tarp on the church roof, when the weather thaws – and it always thaws – we are going to fix that hole. One day, I tell Henry. We will fix that hole. We will shake the generosity tree and raise the funds and replace the roof. We will do it because it needs to be done. We will do it because it's the right thing to do.

And we will do it because of a little girl from the congregation who was born prematurely, weighing only a few pounds – the doctors said she probably wouldn't make it – but her parents prayed and she pulled through and she is now a ball of energy with a grin that could lure the cookies out of the jar. She is at the church almost every night. She skips between the tables for the homeless and lets them rub her head playfully. She doesn't have a lot of toys and she isn't scheduled for countless after-school activities, but she most certainly has a community, a loving home – and a family.

Her father is a one-legged man named Cass, and her mother is a former addict named Marlene. They were married in the I Am My Brother's Keeper church; Pastor Henry Covington did the service.

And a year later, along came their precious little girl, who now runs around as if in God's private playground.

Her name, fittingly, is 'Miracle.'

The human spirit is a thing to behold.

I often wonder why the Reb asked me for a eulogy. I wonder if it was more for me than for him. The fact is, he trumped it moments later.

Just before the cantor began the final prayer, the Reb's grandson, Ron, popped a cassette tape into a player on the pulpit. And over the same speakers where Albert Lewis's voice used to ring out in wisdom, it rang out once more.

'Dear friends, this is the voice of your past rabbi speaking . . .'

He had recorded a message to be played upon his death. He had told no one – except Teela, his shopping companion and health care worker, who delivered the tape to his family. It was brief. But in it, the Reb answered the two questions he had most been asked in his life of faith.

One was whether he believed in God. He said he did.

The other was whether there is life after death. On this he said, *'My answer here, too, is yes, there is something. But friends, I'm sorry. Now that I know, I can't even tell you.'*

The whole place broke up laughing.

I didn't forget about the file on God. I went and retrieved it months later, on my own. I took it off the shelf. When I held it, I actually trembled, because for eight years I'd seen the word 'God' written on the label, and after a while you imagine some holy wind is going to swoosh out.

I looked around the empty office. My stomach ached. I wished the Reb was with me. I yanked it open.

And he was.

Because there, inside the file, were hundreds of articles, clippings, and notes for sermons, all about God, with arrows and questions and scribbling in the Reb's handwriting. And it hit me, finally, that this was the whole point of my time with the Reb and Henry: not the conclusion, but the search, the study, the journey to belief. You can't fit the Lord in a box. But you can gather stories, tradition, wisdom, and in time, you needn't lower the shelf; God is already nearer to thee.

Have you ever known a man of faith? Did you run the other way? If so, stop running. Maybe sit for a minute. For a glass of ice water. For a plate of corn bread. You may find there is something beautiful to learn, and it doesn't bite you and it doesn't weaken you, it only proves a divine spark lies inside each of us, and that spark may one day save the world.

Back in the sanctuary, the Reb concluded his taped message by saying, '*Please love one another, talk to one another, don't let trivialities dissolve friendships . . .*'

Then he sang a simple tune, which translated to:

> '*Good-bye friends, good-bye friends,*
> *good-bye, good-bye,*
> *see you again, see you again, good-bye.*'

The congregation, one last time, joined in.

You could say it was the loudest prayer of his career.

But I always knew he'd go out with a song.

EPILOGUE

One last memory.

This was not long before the Reb passed away.

He was talking about heaven and suddenly, for some reason, I had a notion.

What if you only get five minutes with God?

'Five minutes?' he said.

Five minutes, I said. God is a busy God. Here's your slice of heaven. Five minutes alone with the Lord and then, poof, on you go to whatever happens next.

'And in those five minutes?' he asked, intrigued.

In those five minutes, you can ask anything you want.

'Ah. Okay.'

He pushed back into the chair, as if consulting the air around him.

'First I would say, "Do me a favor, God in heaven, if you can, members of my family who need help, please show them the way on earth. Guide them a little."'

Okay, that's a minute.

'The next three minutes, I'd say, "Lord, give these

to someone who is suffering and requires your love and counsel."'

You'd give up three minutes?

'If someone truly needs it, yes.'

Okay, I said. That still leaves you a minute.

'All right. In that final minute, I would say, "Look, Lord, I've done X amount of good stuff on earth. I have tried to follow your teachings and to pass them on. I have loved my family. I've been part of a community. And I have been, I think, fairly good to people.

'"So, Heavenly Father, for all this, what is my reward?"'

And what do you think God will say?

He smiled.

'He'll say, "Reward? What reward? That's what you were *supposed* to do!"'

I laughed and he laughed, and he bounced his palms on his thighs and our noise filled the house. And I think, at that moment, we could have been anywhere, anybody, any culture, any faith – a teacher and a student exploring what life is all about and delighting in the discovery.

In the beginning, there was a question. In the end, the question gets answered. God sings, we hum along, and there are many melodies, but it's all one song – one same, wonderful, human song.

I am in love with hope.